# INTRODUCTION TO PUBLIC LAW AND HUMAN RIGHTS

## REVISION GUIDE

G000077701

This concise text brings clearly into focus the key elements of public law and human rights. The Q&A approach, examples and exercises provide an excellent way for students to both gain knowledge and apply that knowledge to this complex area of law.

**Dr Ryan Hill**, Deputy Head of School, Anglia Ruskin University, Law School, UK

This resource presents the core framework of Public Law and human rights within the United Kingdom, and also the key current debates surrounding this subject, in clear and accessible language. The technique of using fictional cases to work through practical issues is an excellent way for students to gain insight into the real world application of theoretical principles. Not only does this book help prepare learners for assessments, it also provides support in developing critical legal thinking which will be of great value in their professional lives.

**Javier Garcia Oliva**, Professor of Law, The University of Manchester, UK

# INTRODUCTION TO PUBLIC LAW AND HUMAN RIGHTS

## REVISION GUIDE

### DR ÖZGÜR HEVAL ÇINAR

TRANSNATIONAL PRESS LONDON

2021

Law Series: 3

INTRODUCTION TO PUBLIC LAW AND HUMAN RIGHTS -
REVISION GUIDE
By Dr Özgür Heval Çınar

First published in 2021 by TRANSNATIONAL PRESS LONDON in the United Kingdom, 13 Stamford Place, Sale, M33 3BT, UK.
www.tplondon.com

Transnational Press London® and the logo and its affiliated brands are registered trademarks.

Requests for permission to reproduce material from this work should be sent to: admin@tplondon.com

Paperback
ISBN: 978-1-912997-78-7
Digital
ISBN: 978-1-80135-067-9

Cover Design: Nihal Yazgan

Transnational Press London Ltd. is a company registered in England and Wales No. 8771684

# CONTENTS

# ABBREVIATIONS

APPHL: Associated Provincial Picture Houses Ltd
BoT: Board of Trade
CA: Court of Appeal
CCSU: Council of Civil Service Unions
CMR: Collective Ministerial Responsibility
CPR: Civil Procedure Rules 1998
CRA: Constitutional Reform Act
DA: District Auditor
DM: Decision Maker
DPL: Deo Prakash Limbu
ECHR: European Convention on Human Rights
ECtHR: European Court of Human Rights
ECJ: European Court of Justice
EU: European Union
FCA: Foreign Compensation Act
FCC: Foreign Compensation Commission
FSA: Free Schools Act 2012 (fictitious)
GC: Grand Chamber
GCHQ: Government Communication Headquarters
HCDA: House of Commons Disqualification Act
HO: Home Office
HoC: House of Commons
HoL: House of Lords
HRA: Human Rights Act
IMR: Individual Ministerial Responsibility
KFS: Kent Free School (fictitious)

LCC: Leicester City Council
LGA: Local Government Act
LJ: Law Justice
LTRC: Leicester Tigers Rugby Club
MH: Mardon House
MDB: Milk Distribution Board
MP: Member of Parliament
NAEDHA: North and East Devon Health Authority
NCC: Nottinghamshire County Council
NLBC: Newham London Borough Council
PACE: Police and Criminal Evidence Act
PBC: Poplar Borough Council
PM: Prime Minister
PUV: Procedural Ultra Vires
RAB: Rule Against Bias
RAF: Royal Air Force
RPP: Royal Prerogative Powers
RTAFH: Right to A Fair Hearing
SATs: Standard Attainment Tests
SCA: Senior Courts Act
SoS: Secretary of State
SQE: Solicitors Qualifying Examination
TMBC: Tameside MBC
UDHR: Universal Declaration of Human Rights
UK: United Kingdom
USA: United States of America
WC: Wednesbury Corporation
WDM: World Development Movement

# ABOUT THE AUTHOR

Dr Özgür Heval Çınar is a lawyer. Presently, he is an associate professor at the University of Greenwich, School of Law and Criminology, where he teaches law subjects such as Public Law and Human Rights, English Legal System, EU Law. He completed his PhD at the School of Law, University of Essex. Previously, he was a post-doc fellow at the University of Oxford between 2012 and 2016. In addition, since 2008, he has worked as a legal expert for the Council of Europe, training lawyers, prosecutors, judges, legal officers and legal experts on the European Convention on Human Rights.

# FOREWORD

Public Law and Human Rights is a core module in the legal education of the United Kingdom (UK). Throughout the world it is known as common law. It has reached its present state by incorporating elements of legal sources such as statutes (Acts of Parliament), international law, royal prerogative powers and non-legal sources such as conventions, customs and academic works/opinions.

When it is considered that the UK has three separate jurisdictions – those in England and Wales; Scotland and Northern Ireland – this subject takes on a more interesting and complex state. Hence, all three jurisdictions have their own laws, court structures, lawyers and judges. Nevertheless, laws valid in one jurisdiction, especially those originating from legislation (Acts of Parliament and Statutory Instruments) may have equal, or very similar force, in the other two jurisdictions. Moreover, although courts may hand down different judgments in cases, depending on the jurisdiction, the UK Supreme Court is the highest court for all three jurisdictions. Besides this, the UK was one of the first countries to sign and ratify the European Convention on Human Rights (ECHR) that came into force in 1953, following which it enacted the Human Rights Act (HRA) in 1998, recognising the rights and freedoms embodied in the ECHR in an effective way, shaping the British public law and human rights system and rendering it even more complicated.

Hence, this book will closely examine the public law (constitution and administrative law) and human rights system of the UK (England and Wales in particular). Furthermore, the reason for the emergence of this book is that other publications do not explain such a complex issue in plain language, which makes it very difficult for those taking an interest, in particular A-level as well as LLB/LLM law students. Moreover, experience of teaching this course for many years and particularly knowing the fields in which students experience difficulties, has made me aware of the need for such a work. This book does not repeat material that is available in many textbooks that are in print. Rather, it endeavours to present every topic in plain language and concludes every chapter with a fictitious, explanatory sample case. In other words, it is an introduction to the subject of public law and human rights, the objective of which is to explain the topic both theoretically and in its application. Additionally, this book will assist students to prepare for examinations. At the end of the book there is also a test that summarizes all the subjects contained in the book, which is appropriate to the first stage SQE (Solicitors Qualifying

Examination) examination model that was introduced in September 2021. I hope this book will help all those who have an interest in this subject.

I would also like to express my gratitude to all those at Transnational Press London who provided their full support, and to Prof İbrahim Sirkeci, Mr Andrew Penny, Ms Hülya Ak and to others who contributed that I am unable to name individually here.

**Dr Özgür Heval Çınar**

# PART A

# CONSTITUTIONAL LAW

# CHAPTER I

# INTRODUCTION: THE NATURE AND SOURCES OF THE CONSTITUTION

**Learning Outcomes:**

In this chapter, you should be able to understand:

- ✓ the definition of public law and constitution;
- ✓ the key characteristics of the United Kingdom (UK) Constitution
- ✓ the sources of the UK Constitution
- ✓ the advantages and disadvantages of an (un)written/(un)codified constitution.

**Questions and Answers:**

**1. What is public law?**

The law regarding the relationship between the individual and the State such as constitutional and administrative law.[1]

**2. What is a constitution? Does it have a purpose?**

A constitution is a document that contains rules that members of a society or organisation should follow. In other words, the constitution sets down how a country functions and who is responsible for making the rules.

A constitution has two purposes:

- **Formal purpose**: It founds State institutions and sets out a system of rules and restrictions;
- **Substantive purpose**: A constitution must safeguard fundamental tenets, such as democracy and human rights, so that it may be deemed a constitution.[2]

**3. Why should a State have a constitution at all?**

There are two kinds of theorists who answer this question differently:

- **Formalist theorists**: They believe a constitution should merely establish State bodies and provide a clear framework of rules so that individuals are aware of how they should behave.[3]

---

[1] Çınar, Ö. H., *Introduction to the English Legal System: Revision Guide*, London: Transnational Press London, 2021, p. 8.
[2] Barnett, H., *Constitutional and Administrative Law*, 10th ed., Routledge, 2013, p. 6
[3] Raz, J., *The Authority of Law*, 2nd ed., Oxford University Press, 2009.

- **Substantive theorists**: They believe a constitution should do more than provide a clear framework of rules and should also guarantee basic standards, like democracy and human rights, and safeguard the rights of individuals against both the State and other citizens.[4]

## 4. What are the key features of the UK Constitution?

**Uncodified:** The constitution of the UK is 'uncodified', meaning that it is not based on one official document. Three countries in the world have uncodified constitutions: the UK, Israel and New Zealand.

**Partly written, partly unwritten:** The UK has a partly written and partly unwritten constitution because of the constitutional sources. There are seven sources in total (Please see question 5). Some of these sources are written, such as statutes and case law, whereas other sources are unwritten, such as conventions.

**Constitutional monarchy:** The UK head of State is an unelected monarch with limited powers, as the monarch is not the political head of government. Since 1688 (The Glorious Revolution) power has gradually moved from the monarch to the executive, that is, the government, which is headed by the Prime Minister (PM). The monarch continues to retain formal and ceremonial exercise of powers.

**Flexible:** The UK constitution is flexible, as changes in constitutional sources can be facilitated without difficulty in line with evolving social values. As an example of this, it is straightforward for the UK Parliament to amend legislation, as a simple majority of Members of Parliament (MPs) is all that is required, and the existing electoral system means the Government will have a majority. In comparison, written constitutions are generally more rigid as they were drawn up with the purpose of protecting fundamental rights and freedoms. The Constitution of the United States is a good example of this. In order to change the Constitution in the United States of America (USA), the approval of two-thirds of both chambers of Congress is required, and, subsequently, this proposal must be ratified by three-quarters of the individual States.

**Supreme:** The UK constitution is 'supreme', meaning that the governing institution has unlimited legislative powers. Hence, the Houses of Parliament possesses the highest law-making authority. The powers of a subordinate constitution, in comparison, are restrained by a higher authority.

---

[4] Dworkin, R., *Taking Rights Seriously*, Harvard University Press, 1977; Dworkin, R., *A Matter of Principle*, Harvard University Press, 1985.

**Unitary:** The constitution of the UK is unitary, meaning that the central apparatus of the State holds most of the legal and executive powers. Hence, most power is based in Westminster and Whitehall. Nevertheless, regional authorities are granted certain powers, for instance local authorities (councils); the London Assembly; and, since 1998, the devolved Parliament in Scotland and the Assemblies in Northern Ireland and Wales. In certain areas the devolved nations have substantial, if limited, jurisdiction: these powers came about as a result of Acts of the Parliament in Westminster (i.e., the Scotland Act 1998 and the Government of Wales Act 1998). Since the power to repeal these Acts lies with the UK Parliament, these devolved bodies are legally subordinate to a supreme UK Parliament.

It is worth noting that in States that have a federal constitution, there is a division of powers between national (or 'federal') government and States or provinces. Such States generally possess a constitutional document, for instance, the German and US Constitutions. It is usually the case that certain powers, such as State security and foreign policy, are retained by central government, but the regional authorities (the individual States in the USA or the German 'Bundesländer') are granted substantial powers to introduce legislation and govern themselves.[5]

### 5. How many sources does the UK Constitution have? Can you list them?

The UK Constitution is made up of seven sources based on two main categories:

*Legal Sources (Legally Binding Sources)*

**Acts of Parliament (Statutes):** They are the primary source of the UK Constitution. An Act is a document containing legislation voted on and passed by both Houses of Parliament. There are two types of Acts of Parliament, private Acts and public Acts. A private (or personal) Act of Parliament confers powers or benefits on particular places or people. An example is the Transport for London Act 2016. As for Public (or general) Acts, they are Acts which confer powers or benefits on public concern in general. The European Communities Act (ECA) 1972 or Human Rights Act (HRA) 1998 are examples.

---

[5] BPP Law School, *Study Note on Constitutional and Administrative Law*, BPP Law School, 2018, pp. 6, 12-13; Barnett, p. 10.

**Case Law:** Court judgments in cases of litigation. For instance, ***Entick v. Carrington 1765*** is a case often cited as a landmark case in the consolidation of civil liberties in English law.[6]

**Royal Prerogative Powers:** The term Royal Prerogative Powers in essence refers to powers that were previously exercised by the monarch, but now 'legally' left in the hands of the Crown.

**International Law:** The UK is a dualist State, meaning that international treaties only have effect in domestic law when they are made part of domestic legislation. For example, European Union (EU) Treaties were introduced to domestic law by the ECA 1972. In other words, the ECA provided for the direct applicability of EU law in the UK until the UK left the UK on 31 January 2020.

Similarly, the European Convention on Human Rights (ECHR) was made part of domestic law by the HRA 1998. The Convention was the first document to enshrine a number of the rights contained in the Universal Declaration of Human Rights (UDHR) and make them binding. In other words, this Convention was designed to protect human rights, democracy and the rule of law. The Convention has been updated and more rights have been added to the original text since 1950. At present there are 15 additional protocols.

## *Non-Legal Sources (Not Legally but Morally Binding Sources)*

**Conventions:** Conventions are agreements that are morally, but not legally, binding rules of constitutional conduct. While conventions are sometimes recognised by courts, they are never legally enforced ***(AG v. Jonathan Cape 1975)***.[7]

**Customs:** Customs are rules of conduct that the judiciary recognise as binding. These are rules pertaining to the functions, procedures, privileges and immunities of the Houses of Parliament. Some of these customs are in regulations and standing orders, while others are unwritten and depend on informal understanding and consent. Each House of Parliament has its particular customs and the courts have no jurisdiction over them.

**Academic works/opinions:** In judgments courts regularly make reference to works of academics and writers, whose opinions are valued. For instance,

---

[6] *Entick v. Carrington* [1765] EWHC KB J98.
[7] *AG v. Jonathan Cape* [1975] 3 Alle ER 484.

Dicey's book, entitled 'An Introduction to the Study of the Law of the Constitution'.[8]

## 6. What distinguishes the UK's constitution from those of most other countries?

In the UK:

- The absence of a codified constitution;
- There is no constitutional court. That is, there is no body that carries out a constitutional review of primary legislation (contrast with USA, see *Marbury v Madison, 5 U.S. (1 Cranch) 137 [1803]*);
- More dependence on morally, but not legally, binding 'rules', based on conventions;
- The retention of prerogative powers over numerous important executive responsibilities, which is unusual (defence, foreign policy, treaties etc.);
- A more integrated, traditional institutional structure. A structure that is very different to presidential systems like those in the USA and France, where the President wields executive political power.[9]

## 7. Which source of the UK Constitution are most obviously unwritten in the literal sense? Why do conventions exist?

Conventions are morally binding but not enforceable legally. According to Dicey, "Conventions, understandings, habits or practices, which, though they may regulate the conduct of officials are not in reality laws at all since they are not enforced by the Courts."[10]

Conventions fill the gaps. In other words, as Jennings stated, they put flesh on the dry bones of the law.[11] They provide the space for the law and the constitution to function by putting in place the necessary components.

Dicey also underlined that conventional rule was a guide: "They are all, or at any rate most of them, rules for determining the mode in which the discretionary powers of the Crown ... ought to be exercised."[12] Hence, they may make rigid legal rules more flexible, which could lead to outcomes that in today's constitutional democracy would be disturbing.

---

[8] Dicey, A. V., An Introduction to the Study of the Law of the Constitution, Macmillan, 1885; See also Gillespie, A. and Weare, S., *The English Legal System*, 5th ed., Oxford University Press, 2015, pp. 25-27; Çınar, p. 16; BPP, p. 10-19; Barnett, pp. 25-39; Clements, R., *Q & A Public Law*, 3rd ed., Oxford University Press, 2020, pp. 4-29.

[9] BPP, pp. 2-8; Barnett, pp. 4-40.

[10] Dicey, pp. 23-24.

[11] Jennings, W. I., *The Law of the Constitution*, 5th ed., University of London Press, 1960, pp. 81-82.

[12] Dicey, pp. 422-423.

Moreover, conventions allow the constitution to evolve and adapt. For example, in the 19th century, as the franchise was broadened, conventions played a significant role in the relationship between the House of Common (HoC) and House of Lords (HoL).

They coordinate relations between the Cabinet and the PM; the same is true between the Government and the Houses of Parliament. For instance, the leader of the party with a majority in the HoC has a right to establish a government.

Conventions also provide a means of control, in making ministers accountable to the Houses of Parliament.

The examples below compare conventions with legal rules and provide the rationale:[13]

| Legal Rule | Convention | Rationale for Convention |
|---|---|---|
| The monarch has the right to agree to or reject legislation. | The monarch will always grant royal assent. | Constitutional democracy. |
| The monarch is responsible for appointing the PM and is able to choose whoever they wish. | The Leader of the largest party in the HoC, with a parliamentary majority, is invited to become PM. | Democracy. |
| Judges are able to support a political party. | Judges are not allowed to be active in politics. | Independence of the judiciary (Separation of Powers). |
| The PM is able to exercise prerogative powers over UK armed forces. | It may be argued that the current convention is that for the armed forces to be deployed overseas in sizeable numbers, the PM must gain the approval of parliament.<br><br>A debate continues as to whether votes in 2003 (Iraq war) and in 2013 (negative vote regarding Syria bombing) have brought a convention into being. | Importance of political/ parliamentary approval and scrutiny of UK foreign policy and use of military. |
| Scotland Act – Section 28(7) – the UK Parliament has the right to introduce legislation for Scotland. | Sewel Convention. According to this convention, the UK Parliament will not encroach on areas assigned to Scotland without obtaining the approval of the Scottish Parliament. | Upholding devolved powers and abiding by the spirit of devolution. |
| If it wishes, the opposition in the HoL can express opposition to any government bill. | The Salisbury Convention makes clear that the Lords will not reject a bill which includes a commitment made in a party manifesto. | Respect for the government's democratic mandate in the HoC. |
| Royal family's role (communication with Government). | This is a complex matter to interpret, but an example to focus on is the apparent | It is intriguing that the Attorney General considered the Prince of Wales had a perfect right to learn |

---

[13] BPP, pp. 13-18.

convention that the heir to the throne has the right to learn how the government works. This was the very convention that the Attorney General cited when refusing the freedom of information request by Rob Evans to have access to letters sent by the Prince of Wales to various government ministers **(R(Evans)** v. **Attorney General [2015] UKSC 21)**.

about and influence Government policy, while the convention as regards the Queen is that she should remain completely above all political issues.

## 8. Should constitutional conventions be codified (i.e. put on a statutory footing and given the same status as laws)?

While some arguments in favour of conventions being codified are put forward:

- Certainty and clarity would result;
- The judiciary would be able to enforce them legally;
- Conventions are born of good ideas that have a positive impact on situations, therefore it is rational to grant them legal status;
- At the moment, they depend too much on a sense of fair play.

On the other hand, there are also arguments against the codification of conventions:

- Providing conventions with the same force as laws would damage their flexibility;
- Since conventions come into being according to circumstances, and become redundant in the same way, efforts at codification would involve frequent updating;
- Conventions often concern sensitive political issues (e.g. restricting the functions of the monarch), in which codification could result in a constitutional crisis.[14]

## 9. What are 'Royal Prerogative Powers'? Giving examples, consider the relationship between these powers and statute.

Dicey offers the following definition: "The residue of discretionary or arbitrary authority, which at any given time is legally left in the hands of the Crown."[15] That is, Royal Prerogative Powers (RPP) are powers that were previously exercised by the monarch, which are now 'legally' permitted to remain with the monarch.

---

[14] BPP, pp 13-18; Clements, p. 14.
[15] Dicey, p. 424.

In modern times, most RPP are exercised by Ministers, particularly the PM, acting on behalf of the Crown, rather than the monarch. This has come about on account of the increasing power of elected politicians in the years since 1688, in order to fill the vacuum left by the waning of the monarchy's authority. The prerogative of mercy and the prerogative power relating to the signing of treaties and the declaration of war are examples of prerogative powers.

It is important to note that no new RPP can be created, nor can existing RPP be broadened or extended.[16]

### The Case of Proclamations [1611] 12 Co Rep 74

- Prominent Chief Justice Coke endeavoured - even at a time when the monarch still retained real power - to ensure the King's legal powers remained within legal limits;
- Coke's opinion was that King (James I) could only use the prerogative powers which were already accepted by courts, and that he should not grant himself new ones:
  'The King hath no prerogative but that which the law of the land allows him.'

Therefore, **The Case of Proclamations** entrenched the principle that:

**(i)** The judiciary is entitled to examine the extent of RPP held by the monarch personally. It may be argued that this was the starting point in a long process that culminated in judicial review of these powers established in **GCHQ 1984**;

**(ii)** It was for Parliament, not the monarch, to enact law. This consolidated the view of RPP that has for a long time been seen as residual.

### BBC v. Johns [1965] 1 Ch 32 CA, 79

- The judiciary emphasised that:

**(i)** It is for courts to decide if a RPP exists.

**(ii)** The Crown cannot broaden the extent of an existing RPP:

Lord Diplock commented that "It is 350 years and a civil war too late for the Queen's courts to broaden the Royal Prerogative. The limits within which the executive government may impose obligations or restraints upon citizens of the United Kingdom without any statutory authority are now well settled and incapable of extension... Today, save in so far as the power is preserved by the Statute of Monopolies, or

---

[16] Barnett, p. 88; Clements, pp. 51-70.

created by other statutes, the executive government has no constitutional right either itself to exercise through its agents or to confer upon other persons a monopoly of any form of activity."

## A SAMPLE ESSAY TYPE QUESTION:

**What would be the advantages and disadvantages were the UK to follow most other countries in the world – such as the USA – and adopt a written (or codified) constitution?**

It has never really been necessary for the UK to start afresh or make a break from the past, something that would warrant the writing of a new constitution.

On the one hand, there might be some advantages if the UK were to adopt a written constitution:

- The clear definition of the responsibilities and functions of each branch of State would ensure a proper separation of powers between the three branches of State: the legislature, executive and judiciary.
- Such a system would make sure one branch did not have too much power. For instance, in the USA there are counter balances to the Executive, such as preventing the President from sitting in Congress. The fact the President may only 'suggest' bills to Congress. Similarly, Congress, if it achieves a certain majority, is able to quash a presidential veto of legislation, whereas in the UK the Government can be domineering in the Houses of Parliament (Lord Hailsham's 'elective dictatorship').[17]
- It would bolster the judiciary's hand against executive high-handedness. For instance, the US Supreme Court has made significant constitutional judgments and is able to revoke both Presidential acts and Congressional legislation on the grounds that they are unconstitutional.
- The values of the State could be enshrined – a document of fundamental principles or high standards would create a yardstick against which other legislation could be judged.
- An unambiguous statement of citizens' civil liberties and their rights would be established, preventing Government encroachment – such as the fundamental rights of US citizens enshrined in the US constitution (e.g. the first amendment protects freedom of speech).

---

[17] The elective dictatorship is also called as executive dominance which was used by Lord Hailsham in 1976.

On the other hand, there might be some disadvantages if the UK were to adopt a written constitution:

- Flexibility and the capability of adapting rapidly to changing social mores would be lost. A striking example of this in the USA is the fact that attempts to introduce legislation to restrict access to guns has been stymied by the 'right to bear arms' contained in the Bill of Rights. A right was relevant when the newly-established US needed a civilian militia to oppose foreign intervention, but no longer has any practical relevance.

- In the current UK Constitution, nothing is set in stone, and, therefore, in Bogdanor's words, "saved from being bound by the preconceptions of our forebears."[18] Bogdanor and others argue that a written constitution has never been necessary on account of the fact we believe in the principle of the sovereignty of the Parliament in Westminster (the idea that Parliament may enact whatever legislation it likes and is superior to all other institutions). Bogdanor also maintains that there is no good reason to have a written constitution, as the justification for such a document would be to restrict the powers of a sovereign Parliament.

- The Judiciary might have too much power, resulting in the courts quashing legislation or finding government actions unconstitutional.

- Politicisation of the Judiciary and judicial appointments might be a consequence of a written constitution, and this would harm the independence of the judiciary.

- Excessive obstacles in the name of counter-balances could cause deadlock if the government lost its majority in the Parliament.

- It might result in an end to the flexibility of constitutional conventions.

- In the UK Parliamentary system, it is not easy to detach the Executive from the Legislature, which the US Presidential system can achieve. Hence, a written constitution would inevitably entail a more presidential form of government.

- It is possible to argue that the UK Constitution is firmly founded and does not need to be changed (Think about the following questions: Doesn't the HRA 1998 protect the rights and freedoms of individuals? Aren't the basic tenets of the UK Constitution already in place?).

---

[18] Bogdanor, V., *The New British Constitution*, Hart Publishing, 2009.

# CHAPTER II

# FUNDAMENTAL CONSTITUTIONAL PRINCIPLES

**Learning Outcomes:**

In this chapter, you should be able to understand:

- ✓ the key characteristics of Responsible Government;
- ✓ the key characteristics of the Separation of Powers;
- ✓ the key characteristics of the Rule of Law;
- ✓ the key characteristics of Parliamentary Supremacy.

**Questions and Answers:**

## 1. What is Responsible Government (Ministerial Responsibility)?

Ministerial Responsibility is a constitutional convention which helps to ensure that the Government acts responsibly.[19]

## 2. What are the types of Ministerial Responsibility?

Individual Ministerial Responsibility (IMR) means Government Ministers are held accountable for their actions so that they do not misuse their powers. They are also expected to behave properly in their private lives. In recent times there have been resignations due to infringements of IMR:

- David Blunkett in 2004 rushed through a visa for his ex-lover's nanny, thereby abusing his position as Home Secretary;
- David Laws in 2010 infringed expenses rules by paying his partner £40,000 in rent;
- Liam Fox in 2011 permitted his friend, Andrew Werritty, to pose as a government advisor and attend important Ministry of Defence meetings.

Collective Ministerial Responsibility (CMR) exists so that the Government as an entirety continues to enjoy the confidence of Parliament, and can be held accountable by Parliament for its actions. CMR has three aspects: confidence, unanimity, and confidentiality. If a minister wants to voice his/her personal

---

[19] Institute of Government, 'Ministerial Accountability', https://www.instituteforgovernment.org.uk/explainers/ministerial-accountability (accessed 30 July 2021).

opinion, this minister has to resign.[20] For instance, Clare Short resigned from the Government of Tony Blair in 2003 over the Iraq War, saying:

> I am ashamed that the UK Government has agreed the resolution that has been tabled in New York and shocked by the secrecy and lack of consultation with departments with direct responsibility for the issues referred to in the resolution.[21]

## 3. What is the 2010 Ministerial Code?

The 2010 Ministerial Code (which was most recently updated in August 2019) sets out 'rules' and 'standards' for UK ministers. That is, it bolsters the accountability of UK ministers.[22]

Please note that the Code is only politically (not legally) binding.

## 4. What are the other mechanisms for scrutinising Government?

- Opposition parties (e.g. 30 minutes of Parliamentary Questions to the PM every Wednesday);
- Debates (including emergency debates);
- Select committees (permanent basis);
- Standing committees (temporary basis);
- Votes of no confidence;
- Elections;
- Judicial review;
- Media;
- Standards of public service and openness of Government based on:

  Freedom of Information Act 2000;

  Parliamentary Standards Act 2009.

## 5. What is the Separation of Powers?

Separation of powers is a political doctrine. Aristotle stated: "There are three elements in each constitution in respect of which every serious lawgiver must look for what is advantageous to it; if these are well arranged, the constitution is bound to be well arranged... The three are, first, the deliberative, which

---

[20] BPP, pp. 28-31; Clements, pp. 30-50.
[21] Independent, 'Resignation statement: Errors, secrecy and control freakery - Clare Short's parting shot to Blair', 5 April 2009, https://www.independent.co.uk/news/uk/politics/resignation-statement-errors-secrecy-and-control-freakery-clare-short-s-parting-shot-to-blair-538454.html (accessed 30 July 2021).
[22] Cabinet Office, 'Ministerial Code', https://www.civilservant.org.uk/library/2010_Ministerial_Code.pdf (accessed 30 July 2021).

discusses everything of common importance; second, the officials; and third, the judicial element."[23]

In the UK, the three branches of State are as follows:

- Executive: The Government
- Legislature: Houses of Parliament
- Judiciary: Supreme Court and all other courts

Please note that the monarch is a member of each branch, but the role is symbolic/ceremonial.

A degree of overlap may exist between these branches, with one branch influencing another. The main aim is to ensure that checks/balances will result in the other two branches preventing any one branch exceeding or misusing its powers. That is, the purpose of the separation of powers is to make sure that one branch does not hold more power than is warranted and does not act in an unreasonable way.

The problem in the UK is that because there is no written and/or codified constitution, there is no formal separation of powers between the three branches of State. Existing separation has come into being in an irregular, gradual way. In spite of some overlaps between these branches, effective check/balance mechanisms have been established over time:[24]

## Executive and Legislature

| Overlap | Checks and Balances |
|---|---|
| The 'First past the post' electoral system provides the Government with a ready majority in the Commons – '*elective dictatorship*'? – ensuring most of its programme is implemented. | House of Commons Disqualification Act (HCDA) 1975, Section 1 states that civil servants and members of the police and armed forces cannot be MPs. Individual and collective ministerial responsibility means Government Ministers are held accountable to the Houses of Parliament. |
| Nearly all Government Ministers are MPs or members of HoL. | HCDA 1975, Section 2 states that a maximum of 95 Government Ministers can sit and vote in the HoC at the same time. Ministers are also held to account with questions (written/oral), in debates and in select committees. |
| As most bills are proposed by Government Ministers, Government has effective control of Parliamentary timetable. | The HoC does not have much power to examine delegated legislation. |

[23] Aristotle, *The Politics*, Book iv, xiv, Section 1297b35.
[24] BPP, pp. 35-47; Barnett, pp. 85-86.

| The monarch – member of both executive and legislature (but only with a ceremonial role). | HoC has few powers to look at certain elements of royal prerogative powers (e.g. national security). |

## Executive and Judiciary

| Overlap | Checks and Balances |
| --- | --- |
| Monarch – member of both branches (but only has a ceremonial role). | Judicial review – prevents ministers from exceeding/abusing statutory powers, or justiciable Royal Prerogative Powers (judicial review only examines legality, not merits). |
| Administrative tribunals – appointed by Executive but with a judicial function. | A consolidated fund meets judicial salaries (immune from political interference). The Constitutional Reform Act (CRA) 2005 brought in a system of judicial appointment that functions through the Judicial Appointment Commission. |
| Potential for the judiciary to be politicised through the Lord Chancellor. | The Lord Chancellor is now not head of the judiciary (The CRA 2005 introduced the position of Lord Chief Justice). Judges have immunity from civil suits and protection from contempt laws. A convention exists to the effect that Government Ministers shall not criticise judges. Senior judges possess 'security of tenure'. |

## Legislature and Judiciary

| Overlap | Checks and Balances |
| --- | --- |
| The judiciary has a quasi-legislative role in the evolution of common law and the interpretation of statute. | HCDA 1975, Section 1 stipulates that judges shall not be MPs. |
| Theories of 'judicial law-making': <br> • Declaratory; <br> • Legislative; <br> • Restraint. | The convention is that MPs do not criticise judges. Moreover, judges endeavour to avoid making political comments. Houses of Parliament can change law if it does not concur with developments in common law. |
| Monarch – member of both branches (but only ceremonial role). | Sub-judice rule: Houses of Parliament shall not debate matters relating to pending legal proceedings. Bill of Rights 1689 protects freedom of speech in the Houses of Parliament (part of parliamentary privilege). |
| HoL previously acted as a judiciary as well as a branch of the legislature. | The CRA 2005 introduced a Supreme Court replacing the HoL (Judiciary aspect). Law Lords were replaced by the Supreme Court. Justices of Supreme Court will not become Lords. |

## 6. What is the impact of the Constitutional Reform Act (CRA) 2005 in terms of separation of powers?

The CRA 2005 has consolidated rather than weakened the separation of powers in the UK. For instance, the CRA 2005 accentuated separation between the Government and Judiciary by introducing the Judicial Appointments Commission; and removing the Lord Chancellor from his position as head of the judiciary.

The Supreme Court was established to replace the HoL. This has dealt with the anomaly of 'Law Lords' serving both as judges and as members of the Legislature. Furthermore, the Lord Chancellor lost the position of speaker of the HoL. Moreover, the Lord Chief of Justice became the head of the judiciary in England and Wales, replacing the Lord Chancellor.[25]

## 7. What is the Rule of Law?

Aristotle mentioned the ideal of the rule of law, saying:

> It is better for the law to rule than one of the citizens… so even the guardians of the laws are obeying the laws.[26]

Dicey also stated the key principles of the rule of law as follows:

- Regular law is supreme over arbitrary power. It means that punishment can only be permitted where proven in court that law broken.
- Everybody equal before law. It means that nobody is above law, so courts treat everyone equally.
- There should be no higher law other than rights of individuals, as determined through courts. It means that courts provide remedy for any breach of legal rights.[27]

## 8. What do formalist and substantive theorists believe to be the requirements of the rule of law?

Formalist theorists, like Joseph Raz and John Rawls, believe the rule of law only requires the provision of a clear framework of laws in order that individuals can be sure of their position. They stress the importance of formality, certainty, and

---

[25] This Act came into force in 2009. See the Act at https://www.legislation.gov.uk/ukpga/2005/4/contents
[26] Aristotle, Book iii, Section 1287.
[27] Dicey, Part II, pp. 107-276.

equality in law, but do not accept the possibility that a corrupt State might impose repression on its people using evil and unjust laws.[28]

However, substantive theorists, like Lon Fuller and Ronald Dworkin, are of the opinion that the purpose of the rule of law involves more than establishing a clear framework of laws, arguing that it should also have an 'internal morality' and protect individuals against the State and fellow citizens. That is, the law itself should have consistent moral principles, in particular, justice and fairness. The legitimacy of law depends on its substance, or quality, not solely on the process by which it is introduced.[29]

Apart from the above-mentioned theorists, former Law Lord Thomas Bingham is an influential modern commentator. He spoke about the rule of law at an event at Cambridge University in 2006. He listed eight sub-rules of the rule of law:

1. Law should be accessible, clear and predictable;
2. Legal issues should, ordinarily, be resolved through legal processes, not through exercise of (administrative) discretion;
3. Law should apply equally to all;
4. Law should afford adequate protection for human rights;
5. There should be access to justice in courts without inordinate delay or expense;
6. Public officials, including ministers, should exercise powers they have been granted in good faith, and within the limits of those powers;
7. Legal and adjudicative processes should be fair;
8. The State should comply with its obligations under international law.[30]

## 9. What are the key cases in the rule of law?

### *Entick v. Carrington [1765] 19 St Tr 1029*

This case is important as the judiciary spoke out against the executive during a time, over 250 years ago, when there was great deference to the establishment.

---

[28] Raz, *The Authority of Law*; Rawls, J., *A Theory of Justice*, Oxford University Press,1973 (revision ed. 1999).

[29] Fuller, L., *The Morality of Law*, Yale University Press, 1964; Dworkin, *Taking Rights Seriously*; Dworkin, *A Matter of Principle*.

[30] Law Lord Thomas Bingham, 'The Sixth Sir David Williams Lecture', https://www.cpl.law.cam.ac.uk/sites/www.law.cam.ac.uk/files/images/www.cpl.law.cam.ac.uk/legacy/Media/THE%20RULE%20OF%2 0LAW%202006.pdf (accessed 30 July 2021); BPP, pp. 51-53.

## Liversidge v. Anderson [1942] AC 206

This case is important as Lord Atkin's dissenting view, which was criticised at the time, is now in line with the modern approach of the judiciary.

## Burmah Oil Co Ltd. v. Lord Advocate [1965] AC 75

This case is significant in that it proves that the judiciary, over half a century ago, felt compelled to accept parliamentary supremacy even where the separation of powers and the rule of law had both been breached.

## M v. Home Office [1993] 3 WLR 433

This case is significant as the judiciary confirmed the law applies equally to all and contempt of court applies even to the Home Secretary.

## A and Others v. Secretary of State for the Home Department [2004] UKHL 56

This case is essential because the judiciary played a very important role in evaluating the legitimacy of administrative power over individuals' rights.

## R (Mohamed) v. Secretary of State for Foreign Affairs [2010] EWCA Civ 65

This case is pivotal regarding the control of discretionary power, the importance of equality of arms before the law, and the need for open and transparent justice.

The significance of these cases is that they demonstrate the judiciary is more prepared today to stand up against the executive in time of emergency, although it is a moot point if the war on terror can be compared to World War II.

Considering the above-mentioned cases, the crucial point is that the independence of the judiciary is a fundamental aspect of the rule of law. In the event of the judiciary not being sufficiently independent of other branches of State, there is a risk of arbitrary and oppressive government (in particular as Parliament is dominated by the Government). Although the unwritten constitution of the UK does not explicitly protect judicial independence, the judiciary does enjoy a large degree of independence from other branches of State. However, there is a risk - particularly in cases based on human rights and the application of the proportionality test - that the judiciary may become increasingly politicised, possibly leading to that independence being undermined.[31]

---

[31] Bingham, T., *The Rule of Law*, Penguin, 2011; See also BPP, p. 42, 50-61.

## 10. What is Parliamentary Supremacy?

Parliamentary Supremacy is a legal doctrine which was established in Article ix of the 1689 Bill of Rights.[32] Dicey stated that

> The principle of Parliamentary Supremacy means neither more nor less than this: namely, that Parliament ... has, under the English Constitution, the right to make or unmake any law whatsoever; and, further, that no person or body is recognised by law ... as having a right to override or set aside the legislation of Parliament.[33]

Dicey's definition contains three elements:

- Parliament is the supreme law-making body and may enact or repeal laws on any subject.
- No Parliament may be bound by a predecessor or bind a successor. A particular Act of Parliament cannot be entrenched or given an elevated status.
- No other person or body (but particularly no court of law) may question the validity of an Act of Parliament or declare that Act to be unlawful.[34]

## 11. What are the potential threats to Parliamentary Supremacy?

There are several internal and external threats to parliamentary supremacy as follows:[35]

### *Internal Threats*

### 1. Implied repeal/constitutional statutes

Generally, new Acts of Parliament include phrasing that make clear the Act repeals earlier statutes. However, if a new Act makes no mention of a previous Act and conflict exists in the wording of the two Acts, what happens?

In such cases the doctrine of implied repeal comes into play so that the relevant passage in the new Act implicitly repeals that in the previous Act. This doctrine is in harmony with the principle of parliamentary supremacy as each new Parliament is supreme, therefore the text of the new Act should overrule that of the previous Act.

---

[32] Article ix states that "That the freedom of speech and debates or proceedings in Parliament ought not to be impeached or questioned in any court or place out of Parliament."

[33] Dicey, p. 36 (See also Chapter I, p. 3).

[34] BPP, p. 64; Clements, pp. 96-116.

[35] BPP, pp. 63-81; Barnett, pp. 110-137.

In ***Thoburn 2002***, Laws LJ argued the doctrine of implied repeal is only relevant where the previous Act is 'ordinary' and not 'constitutional'. Laws LJ is of the view that 'constitutional' statutes can only be repealed expressly. However, it is worth noting that Laws LJ's comments were obiter, or 'in passing'. It has yet to be established in a judgment that there is such a thing as a 'constitutional' statute, or that such statutes can only be repealed expressly. Therefore, the Thoburn case would not seem to be a threat to the principle of parliamentary supremacy.[36]

## 2. 'Manner and form' entrenchment

There is general agreement that a new Parliament can amend any existing statute by means of a simple majority. For instance, a previous Parliament cannot entrench an Act by adding a clause stating that the content of the Act can never be altered. However, is it possible to implement entrenchment as regards 'manner and form'? Can a previous Parliament stipulate how an existing Act must be repealed and the form it should take, for instance, by adding the need for a 75% majority and/or the holding of a referendum?

Three judicial decisions ***(Trethowan 1932; Harris 1952*** and ***Ranasinghe 1965)*** which support the 'manner and form' argument have been handed down.[37] In these cases, the conclusion reached was that although a new Parliament cannot be shackled by a previous Parliament as regards the content of an existing statute, a new Parliament can be constricted by a previous Parliament when it comes to the procedure used to amend existing statutes.

But all of the above decisions were handed down by the Privy Council in relation to Commonwealth countries and are therefore only persuasive, not binding in the UK. Hence, there appears to be little threat to parliamentary supremacy from 'manner and form' entrenchment.

## 3. Entrenchment and deference comments

The HoL judgment in ***Jackson 2005***, which endorsed the Parliament Act 1949, and, consequently, the Hunting Act 2004, led to debate of the Parliament Acts 1911/1949, in respect of whether through these Acts, by making it 'easier' for legislation to be enacted, Parliament could also bring in an Act in the future entrenching statute, thus making it 'harder' to legislate.[38]

In the Jackson case the Law Lords' comments did not pose a threat to parliamentary supremacy in that: **(i)** with regard to both entrenchment and

---

[36] Thoburn v. Sunderland City Council [2002] 1 CMLR 50.
[37] Attorney General for New South Wales v. Trethowan [1932] AC 526; Harris v. Minister of the Interior [1952] (2) SA 428 (South Africa); Bribery Commissioner v. Ranasinghe [1965] AC 172.
[38] Jackson v. Attorney General [2005] UKHL 56; [2005] UKHL 56; [2005] 3 WLR 733.

deferral, the comments were merely obiter, hence not part of the judgment; **(ii)** In the judgment itself, the Law Lords deferred to parliamentary supremacy by noting the validity of the Parliament Act 1949 and, thus, the Hunting Act 2004. Hence, parliamentary supremacy does not appear to be under serious threat from the comments of the Law Lords in this case.

## 4. Acts of Union (Scotland 1706-07 and Ireland 1801)

In 1706 the English Parliament passed the Union with Scotland Act. This was followed, in 1707, by the Scottish Parliament passing the Union with England Act.

MacCormick asserted in 1953 that after the passing of these Acts of Union, the English Parliament in Westminster had died and a new UK Parliament had been born, and that this birth was 'unfree' on account of some permanent wording in the Acts.[39]

However, it would be possible to oppose this view by suggesting that it would be a simple task, legally, for Parliament to repeal the Acts of Union with a simple majority. And as there are many more English people than Scots in the UK, a majority of the electorate would probably not disagree with such a repeal. Nevertheless, it was clear in the run up to the 'Scottish referendum in September 2014'[40] that the Government was anxious about the future of the UK. Hence, it might be possible to argue that the Acts of Union poses a challenge to parliamentary supremacy.

## 5. Acts granting independence to former dominions

Once former colonies have gained their independence can the UK Parliament regain its influence?

The argument has been made that the UK Parliament could never reverse statutes granting independence to former colonies. For instance, Lord Denning stated in Blackburn in 1971 that although, legally, such statutes could be repealed easily, there would be no practical effect, adding: "Legal theory must give way to practical politics."[41]

---

[39] MacCormick v. Lord Advocate [1953] SC 396; [1978] 29 NILQ 1.
[40] After agreement was reached between the Scottish and the UK Governments, the Scottish Independence Referendum Bill was introduced on 21 March 2013, passing the Scottish Parliament on 14 November 2013, and receiving Royal assent on 17 December 2013. All residents of Scotland aged 16 and over – more than 4 million people – had the right to vote in the referendum, which took place on 18 September 2014. The question put in the referendum was 'should Scotland be an independent country?' Voters could only answer yes or no. The outcome of the referendum was that 2,001,926 people, 55.30% of those who participated, voted 'No', whereas 1,617.989 people voted for independence, 44.70% of those who took part.
[41] Blackburn v. Attorney General [1971] 1 WLR.

However, in reality, would the UK Parliament want to once again exert influence over former colonies?

As the answer to this question is very likely to be 'no', Independence Acts are not a serious threat to parliamentary supremacy.

## 6. Devolution

By enacting devolution legislation for Scotland, Wales and Northern Ireland in 1998, has the UK Parliament shackled itself for the future?

The devolution legislation has not had a substantive impact on the legal sovereignty of the UK Parliament. As an example,

### Section 28(7) Scotland Act 1998:

> This section does not impinge on the power of the UK Parliament to legislate for Scotland.

However, in reality conventional restraints act as a restraint on the legal power of the UK Parliament. In particular, the **Sewel Convention** means that the UK Parliament should refrain from legislating on devolved matters without the consent of Scotland.[42]

Furthermore, it is noteworthy that the narrow victory for the 'No vote' in the Scottish referendum has focused attention on the vulnerability of parliamentary supremacy. Therefore, it could perhaps be argued that the Devolution Acts are a challenge to parliamentary supremacy, since to repeal them might start a process that concludes with Scotland and Wales leaving the UK. The Scottish referendum highlighted the concerns of both the Government and the main opposition party. Hence, it could also be said that the result of the referendum has made people in Scotland and Wales more aware of their bargaining power. Consequently, the Scottish Parliament and the Welsh Assembly may now be more confident about demanding enhanced devolved powers.

### External Threats

### 7. EU Law

Prior to the UK officially leaving the EU on 30 January 2020, ECA 1972 incorporated EU law into UK law in a robust way that was clearly a threat to parliamentary supremacy. Although Section 2(4) contained no specific reference to the supremacy of EU law, Parliament wording was sufficiently ambiguous for HoL in *Factortame (No. 2) 1991*, with guidance from the

---

[42] Devolution Matters, 'Legislative Consent and the Sewel Convention', https://devolutionsmatters. worldpress.com/the-sewel-convention/ (accessed 30 July 2021).

European Court of Justice (ECJ), to confirm the application of the **Costa v. ENEL 1964** principle that EU law takes precedence over domestic law.[43]

## 8. European Convention on Human Rights (ECHR)

The ECHR appears to constitute very little threat to parliamentary supremacy since the wording of the HRA is weaker than in ECA 1972. For instance, Section 2(1) HRA states that ECtHR decisions must be taken into account – i.e. they are merely persuasive, not binding. And also, Section 3(1) HRA underlines that the UK statute must be interpreted in line with ECHR rights, but only in so far as it is possible to do so. Section 3(2)(b) also highlights that incompatibility does not render UK primary legislation invalid. Finally, Section 4(2) HRA stresses that where UK statute is incompatible with ECHR rights, the UK judiciary can only mention that this is so, and is prevented from invalidating the UK legislation. Section 4(2) states that it is not even an obligation for the UK judiciary to make such declarations, but states it may do so.

A comparison of HoL's (currently Supreme Court) judgments regarding the EU case with HoL judgments pertaining to the ECHR case reveals, as expected, that the ECHR is much less of a threat to parliamentary supremacy than EU law:

In **Factortame (No 2) 1991** the HoL was able to invalidate the sections of the Merchant Shipping Act 1988 which contravened EU law. However, in **A and Others 2004 (Belmarsh case)**, HoL was not able to invalidate Section 23 of the Anti-Terrorism, Crime and Security Act, and could only declare that the Act was incompatible with the ECHR.[44]

However, although it was not incumbent on the UK Government to amend Section 23 of the Anti-Terrorism, Crime and Security Act, it did so. In fact, it is striking that the UK Government has, to date, always opted to amend all clauses of UK statute which the judiciary has found to be in contravention of the ECHR under Section 4. Hence, it would be reasonable to state that the ECHR is a threat to parliamentary supremacy.

## A SAMPLE ESSAY TYPE QUESTION:

"It is one of the great ironies of constitutional law that Montesquieu's theory is in fact based on a misunderstanding of the UK's constitution. ...while recent

---

[43] R v. Secretary of State for Transport, ex parte Factortame Ltd and Others (No. 2) [1991] 1 AC 603; Costa v. ENEL [1964] ECR 585.

[44] A and Others v. SoS Home Dept (Belmarsh case) [2004] UKHL 56

reforms have secured the structural independence of the judiciary, there is a considerable overlap of both personnel and function between Parliament (the UK's legislature, in particular the House of Commons), and Government (the executive). The UK's constitution exhibits a fusion, not a separation, of powers."[45]

**Could you please evaluate the accuracy of Nick Howard's comment?**

**Suggested Answer:**

## Introduction

- Place the question in context by explaining the separation of powers which is a political doctrine concerning the three Powers (or Organs or Branches) of State, namely: Executive - Legislature - Judiciary.
- Explain the aim of the doctrine which is to protect individual liberty against tyranny;
- Before concluding your introduction, you should always explain what you will do in your essay.

## Main Body

- Elucidate the relations between the three bodies (or powers);
- You may want to add substance to your answer and make it easier to read by dealing with the three powers in pairs and dividing the main body of your answer into three subheadings:

  - Executive and Legislature
  - Judiciary and Executive
  - Judiciary and Legislature

An analysis of the following for each pair will help to answer this question: **(i)** the level of separation in that relationship, and **(ii)** the effect of the HCDA and the CRA on this level of separation.

Moreover, you should use relevant case law to broaden your arguments. For this part of the answer, a comparison could be made between: **(i)** cases in which the Judiciary has accepted the importance of respecting the separation of powers; and **(ii)** cases in which the Judiciary has to all intents and purposes ignored the separation of powers.

---

[45] Howard, N., *Beginning Constitutional Law*, 2nd ed., Routledge, 2016, p. 21.

## (i) Cases where the Judiciary has acknowledged the importance of respecting the separation of powers

### Malone v. Metropolitan Police Commissioner [1979] Ch 344; [1979] 2 All ER 620

- Malone, an antiques dealer, was acquitted on a charge of handling stolen goods;
- Evidence emerged that police had tapped his telephone after a warrant was issued by the Home Secretary;
- Malone asked the court to declare phone tapping was unlawful;
- However, because at that time no common law or statutory protection for privacy existed, Malone's request was turned down;
- The High Court (Chancery Division) declared that it was not the courts' role to encroach on the territory of the Legislature by creating a right to privacy where none had previously existed in English law.

### Council of Civil Service Unions v. Minister of State for the Civil Service (the GCHQ case) [1985] AC 374; [1984] 3 All ER 935

- Pertaining to a prerogative power, Minister for the Civil Service (PM Margaret Thatcher) gave oral instructions to trade unions that represented civil servants employed by the Government Communication Headquarters (GCHQ) in Cheltenham. These instructions changed the conditions of service, prohibiting civil servants employed there from being members of trade unions;
- Previous practice had been that the PM would consult the unions at GCHQ prior to making such changes, but Thatcher was concerned that industrial action at GCHQ might compromise national security;
- HoL made two judgments:
  • Exercise of RPP by a PM is not protected from judicial review as it is the Judiciary's constitutional function to interpret and apply law, and to determine the extent of executive discretion under RPP, not the PM's.
  • The PM's failure to consult when using this power contravened rules of natural justice as the previous norm was to consult trade unions before any changes to conditions of employment. This had created a reasonable expectation of consultation prior to any changes that might be made.

The first decision is the key one as far as the separation of powers is concerned since the HoL made clear that it is for the Judiciary, in fulfilling their constitutional function of interpreting and applying the law, and not the Executive, to determine the extent of executive discretion under the RPP. Despite this, the HoL still came down on the side of the PM, but only on account of the needs of national security outweighing the requirement to concur with natural justice.

## *M v. Home Office [1994] 1 AC 377; [1993] 3 WLR 433; [1992] 4 All ER 97; [1993] 3 All ER 537, HL*

- M, a teacher from Zaire, had arrived in the UK in Sept 1990 seeking asylum;
- In spite of medical evidence, M's claim that he had been tortured in Zaire was rejected;
- M's lawyer obtained a court order suspending deportation pending a judicial review;
- However, Home Secretary Kenneth Baker allowed M's deportation to take place and then failed to respect a mandatory court order to return M to the UK from France (where he had been stopped *en route*);
- M was subsequently sent back to Zaire from France, after which he vanished;
- The Home Secretary was found to be in contempt of court;
- The HoL's decision in this case is an illustration of Separation of Powers and the Rule of Law with an independent Judiciary, carrying out its primary function of impartially invoking the law against a senior member of Government;
- Lord Templeman commenced his speech by emphasising the key role of the Separation of Powers in the UK Constitution: "My Lords, Parliament makes the law, the Executive carry the law into effect and the Judiciary enforce the law."

## *R v. Secretary of State for the Home Department ex parte Fire Brigades' Union and Others [1995] 2 WLR 1; [1995] 2 All ER 244; [1993] 3 WLR 433*

- The Home Secretary cited RPP when introducing his own compensation scheme for victims of crime instead of the more generous scheme that had been approved by Parliament;
- HoL declared that the Home Secretary had exceeded his powers by thwarting the will of Parliament. This judgment demonstrates how courts, through judicial review, express their independence as a body which not only applies the law, but also performs a role of monitoring the boundary between Parliament and the Executive;
- The Executive has an obligation to invoke the will of the Legislature and it is up to the Judiciary to ensure the Executive fulfils this role.

### *A and Others v. SoS Home Dept (Belmarsh case) [2004] UKHL 56*

- The appellants in question were certified by the Home Secretary under Section 21 of The men were held in HMP Belmarsh under Section 23 of this Act, which permitted the holding in custody of 'suspected international terrorists', if they could not be deported;
- There was agreement that the persons could not be deported due to a risk of torture in the event they were returned to their countries of origin (hence, it would have been unlawful to deport);
- The Home Secretary issued a 'derogating order' under Section 23. The derogation concerned Article 5(1)(f) of the ECHR, which allows a person to be detained prior to deportation;
- The derogation order declared the grounds for the derogation was the 'terrorist threat to the UK from persons suspected of involvement in international terrorism';
- The Law Lords issued a quashing order pertaining to the Derogation Order and a declaration under Section 4 of the HRA 1998 to the effect that Section 23 of the Anti- Terrorism, Crime and Security Act 2001 contravened Articles 5 and 14 of the ECHR. The HoL's decisions on each of the three points may be interpreted in a way which implies respect for the political doctrine. It is also worth noting that Lord Hoffman's dissenting opinion – arguing there was no emergency that threatened the life of the nation – appeared to contradict the principle of Separation of Powers.

But the majority view regarding the first - public emergency - point was mindful of the Separation of Powers. Lord Bingham's statement, to the effect that the more political an issue is, the more appropriate political resolution will be - by the Executive – instead of the judiciary, was particularly noteworthy. The majority considered that the question of whether a public emergency existed was 'very much at the political end of the spectrum'.

### *(ii) Cases where the Judiciary has apparently disregarded the separation of powers*

In order to make your answer more balanced, you could now cite examples of cases where the Judiciary appeared to ignore the tenets of the separation of powers:

## Gillick v. West Norfolk and Wisbech Area Health Authority [1986] AC 112

- The HoL declared that children under sixteen years of age had the right to give their consent for medical treatment without their parents having a say;

- This decision received criticism from those who argued that it was a significant social and ethical issue which is for Parliament (as the democratic forum) to decide;

- Those who disagreed with the decision emphasised that it was for the Legislature - not the Judiciary - to enact or amend law.

## R v. R [1992] AC 599; [1991] 3 WLR 767, HL; Affirming [1991] 2 WLR 1065; [1991] 2 All ER 257, CA; Affirming [1991] 1 All ER 747, Crown Court

- Husband R was charged with raping wife R, in spite of numerous common law authorities claiming it was not legally possible for a husband to rape a wife;

- The Court of Appeal (CA) found that a husband can - as in this case - rape his wife;

- Lord Lane said that "...This is not the creation of a new offence; it is the removal of a common law fiction which has become anachronistic and offensive";

- The HoL upheld the judgment of the CA. However, as stated in Gillick above, is it not for the Legislature - and not the Judiciary – to deal with legislation in line with the separation of powers, even if the decision in question is to be applauded?;

- The HoL took the view that it had merely modernised the law and had not taken issue with any statute. The ECtHR upheld the HoL decision in **SW v. UK** and **CR v. UK 1995**.[46]

## Airedale National Health Trust v. Bland [1993] AC 789

- Tony Bland was a patient in a persistent vegetative state after being caught up in the calamity that took place during the FA Cup semi-final at Hillsborough on 15.04.1989, suffering crushing and severe brain damage;

- The Hospital, supported by his parents, had applied for a court order to allow Bland to 'die with dignity';

- The HoL decided that, although his death would result, the ruling to remove artificial feeding apparatus was lawful;

---

[46] *S.W. v. UK*, Application no. 20166/92, 22 November 1995, para. 34; *C.R. v. UK*, Application no. 20190/92, 22 November 1995.

- Consequently, Bland became the first person in English legal history to be permitted to die by the courts through the withdrawal of life-prolonging treatment, including food and water.

It could be argued that all three of the decisions cited above flout the requirement under the separation of powers. Furthermore, in all these cases, the judiciary was very close to the boundary between valid judicial interpretation in the context of the common law and improper judicial law making and, according to some, high-jacking the legislative function of Parliament.

## Conclusion

- In the same way as in your introduction, you should always mention the person cited (on this occasion, Nick Howard) in your conclusion.
- You should follow this by explaining your stance on the quotation itself, and the reason why (always remember to give the reason). That is, you should make clear what your opinions are when responding to the question and, importantly, explain the basis of your opinions.
- You might suggest, for instance, that Nick Howard's statement that "...The UK's constitution exhibits a fusion, not a separation of powers ..." may be accurate as regards the fact it has neither a rigid nor a formal separation of powers, both because:
  o It is uncodified and hence there is an absence of intentional design and
  o The electoral system in the UK leads to fusion, particularly in the relationship between the Executive and the Legislature.

- However, you might also want to suggest that Nick Howard's statement makes insufficient recognition of the impact of the HCDA and the CRA, since both statutes include provisions which have deliberately reduced the fusion between the three powers.

# CHAPTER III

# HOUSES OF PARLIAMENT AND THE LEGISLATIVE PROCESS

**Learning Outcomes:**

In this chapter, you should be able to understand:

- ✓ the functions of Houses of Parliament;
- ✓ the balance of power between the HoC and HoL;
- ✓ the law-making process in the Houses of Parliament as well as in the devolved Parliaments in Scotland, Wales and Northern Ireland;
- ✓ the electoral process;
- ✓ parliamentary scrutiny.

**Questions and Answers:**

**1. What are the functions of the HoC and HoL?**

The main functions of the Houses of Parliament are to:

- Check and challenge the work of the Government (scrutiny);
- Make and change laws (legislation);
- Discuss the important issues of the day (debating);
- Check and approve Government spending (budget/taxes).[47]

Parliament is made up of three central elements: The Monarchy, the House of Commons (HoC) and the House of Lords (HoL).

**The Monarch**, as the head of State, takes on constitutional and symbolic duties which have evolved over nearly a thousand years. Besides these State duties, the Monarch has a less ceremonial role as 'Head of Nation'. The Sovereign is a focus for national identity, unity and pride, providing a sense of durability and continuity, formally appreciating success and excellence and supporting the principle of voluntary service.[48]

**The HoC** is the elected chamber of the UK Parliament, enacting legislation and scrutinising the actions of Government. UK voters elect 650 MPs to represent them and their concerns in the HoC. MPs introduce new laws, and

---

[47] UK Parliament, 'What is the role of Parliament?', https://www.parliament.uk/about/how/role/ (accessed 30 July 2021).
[48] Royal UK, 'The role of the Monarchy', https://www.royal.uk/role-monarchy (accessed 30 July 2021).

are able to monitor government policies by putting questions to ministers both in the Commons itself or in Committees.[49]

**The HoL** is the second, unelected chamber of the UK Parliament, with nearly 800 members. It has an important role in examining bills, questioning government actions and investigating public policies.[50]

## 2. What is the balance of power between the HoC and HoL?

The work of the two chambers is similar: framing legislation, monitoring the actions of the government (scrutiny), and discussing topical matters. However, the HoC also has the responsibility of approving Bills that provide money to the government through raising taxes. The general rule is that decisions made in one chamber have to be confirmed by the other.[51]

Prior to the Parliament Act 1911, the HoL had equal power with the Commons regarding legislation, with the exception of the Budget, which deals with monetary issues, that, by convention, the Lords agreed was a matter for the elected chamber. The friction between the HoC and HoL culminated in the Parliament Act 1911, which passed both chambers, but only after the Government threatened to create more peers to ensure the legislation went through. The Act abolished the Lords' right to reject bills dealing with budgetary matters (Money Bills), and introduced a one-month time limit for the Lords to consider such Bills and propose amendments. If the Bill had not been debated and approved without amendment within one month, the Bill would have received royal assent without Lords' approval. Not all financial Bills are Money Bills. Regarding non-Money Bills, the power of the HoL was curbed, with their right to reject legislation watered down and replaced by a power to delay Bills for a two- year period spread over three parliamentary sessions. This right was further reduced by the Parliament Act 1949 which shortened the HoL' power of delay over non-Money Bills from two years to one year. The Parliament Act 1911 regarding Money Bills passed with no amendments being made.[52]

---

[49] UK Parliament, 'House of Commons', https://www.parliament.uk/business/commons/ (accessed 30 July 2021).
[50] UK Parliament, 'Work of the House of Lords', https://www.parliament.uk/business/lords/work-of-the-house-of-lords/ (accessed 30 July 2021).
[51] UK Parliament, 'The two-House system', https://www.parliament.uk/about/how/role/system/#:~:text=Their%20work%20is%20similar%3A%20making,approving%20Bills%20that%20raise%20taxes (accessed 30 July 2021).
[52] Barnett, pp. 356-357.

## 3. What types of legislation are there in England and Wales?

| Primary Legislation | Secondary Legislation (also known as Delegated Legislation) |
|---|---|
| Acts of Parliament. There are two kinds:<br>• Private (Personal) Act;<br>• Public (General) Act. | • Statutory Instruments;<br>• Byelaws;<br>• Procedural Rules;<br>• Orders in Council. |

## 4. Explain Acts of Parliament

An Act of Parliament is a document containing legislation voted on and passed by Parliament.

There are two types of Acts of Parliament, private Acts and public Acts. A private (or personal) Act of Parliament confers powers or benefits on particular places or people. An example is the Transport for London Act 2016.

As for Public (or general) Acts, they are Acts which confer powers or benefits on public concern in general. The ECA 1972 or HRA 1998 are examples.[53]

## 5. Explain secondary (delegated) legislation

Secondary (also known as delegated) legislation is a term used to describe law made by ministers (or other bodies), with powers provided by an Act of Parliament.[54]

**Statutory Instruments (SIs):** SIs are the main form in which secondary legislation is introduced in the UK. An Act of Parliament provides the power to make a statutory instrument and is usually conferred on a Minister of the Crown, who can then introduce the relevant secondary legislation mentioned in the Act. SIs may follow affirmative or negative procedure, or have no procedure at all, but the Act stipulates which to use.[55]

**Byelaws:** Byelaws are laws made by a local council in accordance with power in a public general act or a local act which requires action in a particular area. These laws come with sanction or penalty if they are not complied with.[56]

**Procedural Rules:** Rules on procedure constitute a procedural code, the main aim of which is to ensure courts handle cases in the proper way.[57]

---

[53] Gillespie and Weare, pp. 25-27.

[54] UK Parliament, 'Delegated legislation', https://www.parliament.uk/site-information/glossary/delegated-or-secondary-legislation/ (accessed 30 July 2021).

[55] UK Parliament, 'Statutory instruments (SIs)', https://www.parliament.uk/site-information/glossary/statutory-instruments-sis/ (accessed 30 July 2021).

[56] 'Guidance: Local government legislation byelaws', https://www.gov.uk/guidance/local-government-legislation-byelaws#introduction (accessed 30 July 2021).

[57] Justice, 'Procedure rules', http://www.justice.gov.uk/courts/procedure-rules (accessed 30 July 2021).

**Orders in Council:** Orders in Council are a regulation issued by the Queen on the advice of the Privy Council. However, in modern times, orders are only issued following advice from Ministers. The redistribution of functions between Ministers is an example, using powers provided by an Act of Parliament. Another type of order, used to make appointments to the civil service, is issued under the royal prerogative. While Orders in Council require approval by the monarch, the government drafts and controls them.[58]

## 6. What are the advantages and disadvantages of using secondary legislation?

| Advantages | Disadvantages |
|---|---|
| • Saves time;<br>• Produced with specialist knowledge;<br>• Control exercised by Parliament. | • Lack of oversight;<br>• Lack of publicity;<br>• Undemocratic;<br>• Risk of sub-delegation.[59] |

## 7. What is the primary legislation-making process?

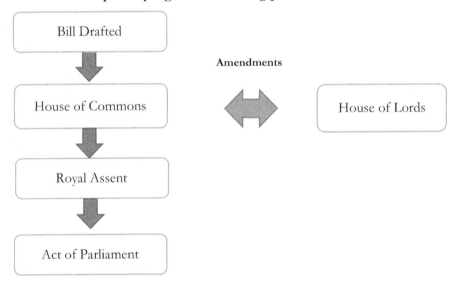

---

[58] UK Parliament, 'Orders in council', https://www.parliament.uk/site-information/glossary/orders-in-council/ (accessed 30 July 2021).

[59] Thomas, M. and McGourlay, C., *Concentrate English Legal System*, Oxford University Press, 2017, p. 33.

**The legislative stages:**[60]

**First Reading:** This is just a formal stage with no debate on the bill.

**Second Reading:** This entails a debate in the chamber on the main features of the bill. A government minister commences the debate by making a case for the bill and explaining the measures it contains. The opposition responds and members are then able to discuss it. The government then draws the debate to a conclusion by answering the points raised.

**Committee Stage:** At this stage the bill is subjected to a line-by-line evaluation. In the Commons a specially convened committee of MPs (a Public Bill Committee), based on the balance of forces in the House, may carry out this evaluation.

**Report Stage:** At this stage, which takes place in the chamber in both Houses, if amendments have been tabled, they are discussed, if not, this is a purely formal stage. Just like in the committee stage, the amendments may alter what is in the bill, or lead to the addition of new provisions.

**Third Reading:** In the Commons this involves another general debate of the bill which usually happens straight after the Report stage (or, if the EVEL procedures apply, immediately after it has been examined by the Legislative Grand Committee). No amendments can be tabled. In the Lords, the Third Reading happens on a later day, and tidying up amendments may be tabled.

**Later stages:** Agreement on the text of a bill is required in both Houses in order for it to become an act. Therefore, if the bill is amended in the Lords, it must be sent back to the Commons for these amendments to be scrutinised. The first House can, if it wishes, reject the amendments, alter them or propose alternatives. Hence, it is quite possible for a bill to move between the two Houses several times before agreement is reached. As a result, this stage is often referred to as 'ping pong'.

**Royal Assent:** After a bill has been passed by both Houses it becomes law once it receives Royal Assent. The bill then becomes an act.

## 8. How does the law-making process work in the devolved countries?

When a law is enacted by the Houses of Parliament, it will come into force in the whole UK, i.e., England, Wales, Scotland and Northern Ireland.

However, since devolution has established a Scottish Parliament, a Welsh Assembly and a Northern Ireland Assembly, substantial powers have been

---

[60] 'Guidance: Legislative process taking a bill through Parliament', https://www.gov.uk/guidance/legislative-process-taking-a-bill-through-parliament (accessed 30 July 2021).

transferred away from the Houses of Parliament to the nations that make up the UK. Nevertheless, authority over the devolved institutions has been retained by the UK Parliament.[61]

This devolved system differs from a federal or confederal system of government in which every part of a State has autonomy. According to the constitutional tradition of 'parliamentary sovereignty' in the UK, devolution can, hypothetically, be reversed. The legislative basis of devolution was set out in the Scotland Act 1998, the Government of Wales Act 1998 and the Northern Ireland Act 1998, although all three have since then been amended. A non-legislative framework of agreements has also been put in place which help resolve disputes between the central and devolved government.

This is an asymmetric system of devolution in that there are different forms of devolution and amounts of power in the different parts of the UK. Scotland, Wales and Northern Ireland all have executive and legislative devolution, while in parts of England Metro Mayors (and the Mayor of London) only possess executive powers. Combined Authorities and the London Assembly are able to check executive decisions but cannot enact laws in the same way as the Scottish Parliament, the Welsh Assembly and the Northern Ireland Assembly.

The three legislatures are only allowed to enact primary and secondary legislation in devolved (or 'transferred' in the case of Northern Ireland) fields, with 'reserved' issues (or reserved and 'excepted' in Northern Ireland) still the responsibility of the UK Parliament. The Parliament can still pass laws in devolved fields, but, according to the Sewel Convention, does 'not normally' do this unless it has the clear consent of the devolved institution in question.[62]

Devolved matters refer to the fields of government that have been delegated by the UK Parliament to the Scottish Parliament, the Welsh Assembly, Northern Ireland Assembly and London or other Local Authorities.[63] These matters include: health and social care, education and vocational training, local government, agriculture, forestry and fisheries, transport, certain areas of taxation, justice and policing, certain aspects of social security, sports and the arts.[64]

---

[61] UK Parliament, 'Devolved Parliaments and Assemblies', https://www.parliament.uk/about/how/role/relations-with-other-institutions/devolved/ (accessed 30 July 2021).

[62] Torrance, D., 'Introduction to devolution in the UK', https://commonslibrary.parliament.uk/research-briefings/cbp-8599/ (accessed 30 July 2021).

[63] UK Parliament, 'Devolved and Reserved Matters', https://www.parliament.uk/site-information/glossary/devolved-and-reserved-matters/ (accessed 30 July 2021).

[64] Civil Service, 'Devolution: Factsheet', https://assets.publishing.service.gov.uk/government/uploads/system/uploads/attachment_data/file/770709/DevolutionFactsheet.pdf (accessed 30 July 2021).

Powers that are reserved for the UK Parliament include the constitution, foreign affairs, defence, trade policy, international development, immigration, nationality and broadcasting (The Northern Ireland may enact legislation with the permission of the Secretary of State).[65]

To sum up, if there is a dispute between UK laws and laws in one of the countries that comprise the UK, UK law has supremacy.[66]

## 9. What is the electoral process for members of the Houses of Parliament?

In the UK the public democratically elect 650 MPs to the HoC. At a general election voting takes place in constituencies. Electors vote by placing a (X) next to their preferred candidate on a ballot paper. Ballot papers are counted and the candidate with the most votes represent the constituency.[67]

As for the HoL, no members are elected. There are several different types of peerages in the HoL:

- Some MPs, of whichever party, are appointed life peers when they depart the HoC at the end of a parliament;
- A PM may recommend peerages when he or she leaves office in 'resignation honours';
- MPs can be appointed to 'top up' the three main party groups in the HoL. These members are expected to attend on a regular basis and act as spokespersons or business managers (whips);
- One-off announcements can take place when someone is appointed as a minister who is not a member of House;
- There are 26 Church of England archbishops and bishops who sit in the House. Their membership ends when they retire as bishops and the next most senior bishop takes their place. The Archbishop of Canterbury is generally made a life peer when he retires;
- It is a tradition that former speakers of the HoC are appointed life peers at the request of the HoC.

The independent House of Lords Appointments Commission was set up in 2000. It recommends individuals to be appointed as life peers without party-political affiliation. It also checks nominations for all life peers, including those from political parties, to ensure they are suitable. Recommendations can also

---

[65] Ibid.
[66] Thomas and McGourlay, p. 4.
[67] UK Parliament, 'Voting Systems in the UK', https://www.parliament.uk/about/how/elections-and-voting/voting-systems/ (accessed 30 July 2021).

be made by the public. After being approved by the PM, appointments are confirmed by the Queen.[68]

## 10. What is parliamentary scrutiny?

Parliamentary scrutiny is the term used to describe the detailed checking and inspection of government policies, actions and spending that is undertaken by the HoC and the HoL and their committees.[69]

The HoC and the HoL scrutinise government policy in similar ways, albeit with different procedures. The main means used are to question government ministers, stage debates and to carry out investigative work through committees. In response, the government explains the reasons for its policies and decisions. The following means of scrutiny exist:[70]

- MPs and Lords can question government ministers in the House during regular oral question times or in writing;
- The PM answers questions every Wednesday when Parliament is sitting from 12.00 noon - 12.30 pm;
- Debates are held in the Commons to give MPs a chance to examine proposed legislation and amendment of laws in addition to questions of a national or international nature. There are often votes taken to establish whether a majority of Members are in favour of or reject the legislation or proposal in question;
- Committees of MPs and/or Lords are given the task of examining specific policy issues or legislation in detail. Different committees undertake different roles, from offering advice, to compiling reports or amending legislation;
- There are departmental select committees in the HoC, that were set up to 'shadow' government departments and examine their spending, administration and policy;
- There are permanent and temporary committees in both houses, and Joint Select Committees in which MPs and Lords work together. The government makes written responses to most committee reports;
- Many questions asked on the floor of either house also receive written replies. Such questions may be quite specific and require a detailed response. An MP is entitled to ask as many questions as they like, there being no limit;[71]

---

[68] UK Parliament, 'How Members Are Appointed', https://www.parliament.uk/business/lords/whos-in-the-house-of-lords/members-and-their-roles/how-members-are-appointed/ (accessed 30 July 2021).
[69] UK Parliament, 'Scrutiny (Parliamentary Scrutiny)', https://www.parliament.uk/site-information/glossary/scrutiny-parliamentary-scrutiny/ (accessed 30 July 2021).
[70] UK Parliament, 'Checking the Work of Government', https://www.parliament.uk/about/how/role/scrutiny/ (accessed 30 July 2021).
[71] BPP, pp. 24-25.

- The Standing Committee has a single member, plus one member from each delegation to the Assembly, who alternates. It regulates the Assembly's programme, verifies its draft budget and oversees the Assembly's permanent secretariat.[72]

## A SAMPLE ESSAY TYPE QUESTION:

Mr Tim Johnson is an MP and Secretary of State for Health. In May, Mr Johnson gets up one morning to see journalists massed outside his constituency home. He discovers that a computer disc from his Department has been found on a train. It is thought a junior civil servant lost it on the way home. The disc contained personal details of all NHS patients in England.

**Please give Mr Tim Johnson advice regarding this scenario.**

**Suggested Answer:**

The loss of NHS patients' confidential information comes under the convention of individual ministerial responsibility (IMR).

The original convention of IMR involving serious error in a department demanded the resignation of the minister concerned. The most-cited 20th century example of a minister accepting personal responsibility for departmental mistakes by resigning is that of Sir Thomas Dugdale in the Crichel Down affair in 1954. In that case the Minister had some knowledge of the activities of the civil servants involved.

Sir David Maxwell Fyfe, who was Home Secretary when the Crichel Down incident occurred, identified four situations in a subsequent report:

1. When a clear order is made by a Minister the minister must stand up for the civil servant who has implemented the order.
2. When the civil servant behaves in accordance with the policy put in place by the minister, the minister is again duty bound to defend the civil servant.
3. An official makes an error or is responsible for some delay, but not in an important matter of policy.
4. When a civil servant has done something which the minister does not approve of and is unaware of, and the official is culpable.[73]

---

[72] UK Parliament, 'Standing Committee', https://www.parliament.uk/mps-lords-and-offices/offices/delegations/nato-pa/nato-pa-committees/standing-committee/ (accessed 30 July 2021).
[73] UK Parliament, 'Chapter 2: Ministerial Responsibility for the Civil Service', https://publications.parliament.uk/pa/ld201213/ldselect/ldconst/61/6105.htm (accessed 30 July 2021).

In situations 1 and 2, the Home Secretary considered that the minister should resign. In situations 3 and 4, he considered the minister does not need to resign on account of not having personal knowledge of the action. This is still, in theory, the crux of the convention.

According to the current interpretation of the convention, the loss of NHS patients' details would come under point 3 and/or 4 of the above guidelines, therefore the minister's resignation would be unlikely to be required (See the similar case of Alistair Darling – who remained in post and did not resign after HM Customs and Excise lost computer discs containing data concerning millions of people in November 2007).[74] This case was regarded as an operational failure, in essence an error, and is a good example of the current interpretation of the convention.

A point that could be raised is whether sufficient precautions had been taken to secure such data. If no rules or procedures existed within the department for safeguarding data (which might contravene the Data Protection Act), this would arguably take the matter into category 2 of Crichel Down – that is, the civil servant (by carrying the disc on to the train) was acting in accordance with policy (in reality, an absence of policy) implemented by the Minister. In this scenario, it might be a contravention of IMR if Mr Johnson fails to resign.

**If IMR and CMR often fail to secure political accountability, what other mechanisms can be utilised to hold the Executive to account?**

The main political mechanisms are:[75]

- Questions
    - Parliamentary questions in written or oral form (to responsible Minister);
    - PM's question time (30 mins every Wednesday);
    - Private notice questions – urgent requests (at the discretion of the Speaker).

- Debates
    - Main business – i.e. debate on legislation (2nd reading) – although the Government can limit this by using the 'guillotine';
    - Opposition Day debates – opportunities for Opposition parties to introduce a critical motion;

---

[74] Patrick Wintour, 'Lost in the post - 25 million at risk after data discs go missing', The Guardian, https://www.theguardian.com/politics/2007/nov/21/immigrationpolicy.economy3 (accessed 30 July 2021).
[75] BPP, pp. 24-27; Clements, pp. 71-95.

- o Emergency debates – unusual, and at Speaker's discretion (See also statements to the House, by the Government – to announce important news);
- o Adjournment debates – regular opportunities for backbenchers (on a ballot system) to bring up important (usually local) matters;
- o Early Day Motions – appeals for debate, but in practice just a means of promoting an issue.

- Committees

  - o **Standing Committees:** They are temporary committees which discuss proposed legislation – i.e. 'committee stage' of a Bill;
  - o **Select Committees:** They are permanent departmental committees that are perhaps the most efficient way for Parliament to hold ministers to account. The work of these committees is now televised and receives quite substantial coverage in quality newspapers. The role of Select Committee Chair is respected and considered a good way to progress for many talented MPs.

Additionally, it is a good idea to explore other ways in which government can be scrutinised:

- o The judiciary does this through judicial review;
- o The media has a very important role in ensuring government and politicians in general behave responsibly. For instance, the Telegraph was prominent in the MPs' expenses scandal and the Guardian exposed links between government and News International and the scandal of the abuse of personal privacy by News International.[76]

---

[76] See 'Exclusive: the real story of the MPs' expenses scandal', The Telegraph, https://www.telegraph. co.uk/news/mps-expenses-scandal/ (accessed 30 July 2021); 'NSA files: Decoded', The Guardian, https:// www.theguardian.com/world/interactive/2013/nov/01/snowden-nsa-files-surveillance-revelations-decoded (accessed 30 July 2021).

# PART B

# HUMAN RIGHTS

# CHAPTER IV

# HUMAN RIGHTS IN THE UK: HUMAN RIGHTS ACT 1998 AND EUROPEAN CONVENTION ON HUMAN RIGHTS

**Learning Outcomes:**

In this chapter, you should be able to understand:

- ✓ the HRA 1998;
- ✓ the ECHR and the ECtHR;
- ✓ the relationship between the HRA 1998 and the ECHR;
- ✓ the fundamental rights, their types and principles;
- ✓ the preliminary requirements for bringing a human rights case.

**Questions and Answers:**

## 1. What is dualism and what are its requirements in the context of human rights?

The UK is a dualist State, meaning that international treaties only have effect in domestic law when they are made part of domestic legislation. For instance, EU Treaties were introduced to domestic law by the ECA 1972. Similarly, the UK Parliament needed to pass its own UK statute to incorporate the ECHR into UK law even after the UK Government had signed the ECHR in 1950.

Almost all European legal systems are monist. This system involves considering all branches of law as being part of a single, binding legal system. If there is any clash between domestic and international law, the international law rule is superior and overrides the domestic rule.[77]

## 2. What was the reason behind the UK enacting the Human Rights Act 1998?

The Human Rights Act received royal assent on 9 November 1998, coming into force on 2 October 2000.

Prior to the HRA coming into force the ECHR was not part of the UK Constitution, although UK citizens had been able to petition the ECtHR since 1966. UK citizens only had residual freedoms, meaning that they were free to do what was left (the residue) after weighing what by law they were prohibited from doing. The situation in the USA is very different, as citizens have had

---

[77] Çınar, p. 35.

positive rights, safeguarded by the US Constitution, for over two hundred years. In the 1990s there were calls for the UK citizens to enjoy similar positive rights to US citizens and the Labour Party under Tony Blair promised to introduce such rights before the election victory in 1997.[78]

### 3. What was the effect of the UK enacting the Human Rights Act 1998?

The HRA brought the ECHR into UK law, establishing it as an additional source in the UK Constitution.

The HRA contains the rights and freedoms of the ECHR. Indeed, each ECHR Article from 2 up to 14 contains a positive 'human right and fundamental freedom' with the additional protocols as follows:

- Right to life (Article 2);
- Prohibition of torture (Article 3);
- Prohibition of slavery and forced labour (Article 4);
- Right to liberty and security (Article 5);
- Right to a fair trial (Article 6);
- No punishment without law (Article 7);
- Right to respect for private and family life (Article 8);
- Freedom of thought, conscience and religion (Article 9);
- Freedom of expression (Article 10);
- Freedom of assembly and association (Article 11);
- Right to marry (Article 12);
- Right to an effective remedy (Article 13);
- Prohibition of discrimination (Article 14);
- Protection of property (First Protocol 1, Article 1);
- Right to education (First Protocol 1, Article 2);
- Right to free elections (First Protocol 1, Article 3).

### Please note that there is no explicit hierarchy of rights in the Convention.

Article 1: The High Contracting Parties shall secure to everyone within their jurisdiction the rights and freedoms defined in Section 1 of this Convention.

Article 13: Everyone whose rights and freedoms as set forth in this Convention are violated shall have an effective remedy before a national authority notwithstanding that the violation has been committed by persons acting in an official capacity.

---

[78] Donald, A., Gordon, J., and Leach, P., *The UK and the European Court of Human Rights,* Equality and Human Rights Commission Research report 83, 2012.

The UK felt the above-mentioned two ECHR Articles did not need to be incorporated because Section 1 of the HRA gives effect to ECHR rights and freedoms in the UK. Therefore, it was decided not to include Article 1. Furthermore, Section 8 of the HRA provides an effective remedy, therefore Article 13 was not included in the HRA.

### 4. What is the European Convention on Human Rights (ECHR)?

The ECHR, also known as the Convention for the Protection of Human Rights and Fundamental Freedoms, was adopted in 1950 and entered into force in 1953. The Convention was the first document to enshrine a number of the rights contained in the UDHR and make them binding. In other words, this Convention was designed to protect human rights, democracy and the rule of law. The Convention has been updated and more rights have been added to the original text since 1950. At present there are 15 additional protocols.

### 5. What does the ECHR contain?

### 6. What are the categories of the HRA/ECHR rights?

**(i) Absolute rights:** Rights that are non-derogable, meaning the State cannot place limitations on them: Articles 3, 4 and 7.

**(ii) Limited rights:** The State can, in some circumstances, legitimately place limits on these rights: Articles 2, 5 and 6. The exceptions to this rule are mentioned in the articles in question (termed 'limitations').

**(iii) Qualified rights:** Articles 8, 9, 10 and 11 are deemed qualified rights. The first paragraph of these articles outlines the right(s) to be protected by the Convention. In the second paragraph these rights are then qualified with information given as to how the State may lawfully impose restrictions.[79]

---

[79] Harris, D. and O'Boyle M., *Harris, O'Boyle & Warbrick: Law of the European Convention on Human Rights*, 4th ed., Oxford University Press, 2018, pp. 108-109.

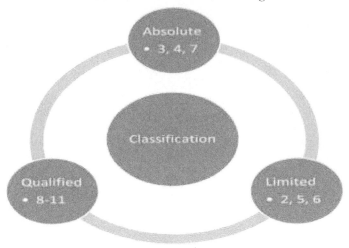

## 7. What does the European Court of Human Rights (ECtHR) do?

The ECtHR implements the ECHR. It has a responsibility to safeguard the rights and guarantees enshrined in the Convention and to ensure compliance by member States.

It accepts complaints (called "applications") made by individuals or, occasionally, by States. When the Court finds that a member State has contravened one or more of these rights, the Court hands down a judgment documenting a violation.[80]

## 8. Are the ECtHR's judgments legally binding on member States?

Firstly, according to Article 1 of the ECHR, "The High Contracting Parties shall secure to everyone within their jurisdiction the rights and freedoms defined in Section 1 of this Convention."

Secondly, according to Article 46(1) of the ECHR, "The High Contracting Parties undertake to abide by the final judgment of the Court in any case to which they are parties."

In sum, the countries concerned are under an obligation to comply with the judgments of the ECtHR. However, the UK introduced HRA 1998 stating clearly in Section 2(1) that UK courts must take ECtHR's case law 'into account' when dealing with issues linked to a right enshrined in the ECHR. It is worthy of note that before the enactment of the HRA in 1998, people in England and Wales wishing to benefit from rights enshrined in the Convention

---

[80] 'European Court of Human Rights', https://echr.coe.int/Pages/home.aspx?p=home (accessed 30 July 2021).

had to go to the ECtHR. Presently, once a victim exhausts all domestic remedies, s/he can still go to the ECtHR.

The first judgment that considered the meaning and scope of Section 2(1) HRA 1998 was *R (Alconbury Developments Ltd) 2001*, a case in which the HoL found that, although ECtHR jurisprudence is not binding, national courts have an obligation to follow any appropriate case law unless there are particular circumstances, or ECtHR judgments leading to an outcome that fundamentally contradicts the apportioning of powers according to the UK constitution.[81]

In *R (Ullah) v. Special Adjudicator 2004*, Lord Bingham made the observations set forth below, with which his fellow judges on the panel concurred:

> [T]he House is required by section 2(1) of the Human Rights Act 1998 to take into account any relevant Strasbourg case law. While such case law is not strictly binding, it has been held that courts should, in the absence of some special circumstances, follow any clear and constant jurisprudence of the Strasbourg court: R (Alconbury Developments Ltd) v Secretary of State for the Environment…, paragraph 26. This reflects the fact that the Convention is an international instrument, the correct interpretation of which can be authoritatively expounded only by the Strasbourg court. From this it follows that a national court subject to a duty such as that imposed by section 2 should not without strong reason dilute or weaken the effect of the Strasbourg case law … It is of course open to member states to provide for rights more generous than those guaranteed by the Convention, but such provision should not be the product of interpretation of the Convention by national courts, since the meaning of the Convention should be uniform throughout the states party to it. The duty of national courts is to keep pace with the Strasbourg jurisprudence as it evolves over time: no more, but certainly no less.[82]

It is also worth noting that Section 3(1) stipulates that courts should interpret statutes thus: "…so far as it is possible to do so, primary legislation and subordinate legislation must be read and given effect in a way which is compatible with convention rights."

Furthermore, courts are within their rights to state that a piece of primary legislation does not comply with the HRA 1998 (Section 4).

---

[81] R (Alconbury Developments Ltd) v. Secretary of State for the Environment [2001] UKHL 23.
[82] R (Ullah) v. Special Adjudicator [2004] UKHL 26, para. 20.

This means that courts have the power to make a declaration of incompatibility.[83]

## 9. What are the preliminary requirements if you would like to bring a claim based on the HRA 1998?

### The public authorities

The defendants against whom they can bring their claims under section 6(1) HRA 1998, UK citizens may bring ECHR claims against public authorities. This section of the HRA states "It is unlawful for a public authority to act in a way which is incompatible with a Convention right."

Courts have identified two sorts of public authority as a result of their interpretation of section 6 HRA:

**(i) Core public authorities:** Section 6(1) applies. These include traditional bodies (which Lord Nicholls mentioned in HoL decision in *Aston Cantlow 2003*), such as the Government, local authorities, or the armed forces, whose public role is so ingrained that they are manifestly public authorities;

**(ii) Hybrid/functional public authorities:** Section 6(3)(b) and Section 6(5) apply. These include organisations, like privatised utility companies, which are less evidently public authorities, but do carry out some public functions *(Leonard Cheshire 2002)*.[84]

This contrast between core and hybrid public authorities is significant as, while core public authorities are always subject to section 6(1) as regards everything they do, hybrid public authorities are only subject to section 6(1) as regards its actions which are considered to be public nature.

Since no definitive test exists for determining hybrid public authorities, the Judiciary makes its decision on the facts before it in each case.

### The location of the court (Jurisdiction)

Prior to the enactment of the HRA, UK citizens had to go to the ECtHR in Strasbourg to pursue ECHR claims.

UK citizens are now able to bring ECHR claims in the domestic High Court in England and Wales (in Scotland there are separate arrangements).

UK citizens are still able to go to the ECtHR, but only after they have exhausted all domestic remedies.

---

[83] Çınar, pp. 41-43.
[84] Aston Cantlow and Wilmcote with Billesley Parochial Church Council v. Wallbank [2004] 1 AC 546; [2003] UKHL 37; [2003] 3 All ER 1213; [2003] 3 WLR 283; Leonard Cheshire [2002] EWCA Civ. 366.

Moreover, it is worthy of note that the HRA 1998 has an extra-territorial application. That is, a claim can be brought for acts that have taken place outside the geographical jurisdiction of a State party. In ***Al-Skeini and others v. UK*** the ECtHR widened the sphere of Convention law to include Iraq, something which the HoL (now Supreme Court) had not done in the domestic case (in 2007). The ECtHR considered that as the British military authorities in southern Iraq were responsible for security in the area in which they were deployed, killings which British soldiers had committed could be considered within its jurisdiction (not only the deaths, such as that of Baha Mousa, which occurred in British military bases).[85]

After this case, the Supreme Court concluded there had not been a violation of Article 2 in the case of ***R (Smith) 2010***.[86] In this case Private Jason Smith, a Territorial Army soldier, had died of heatstroke while in Iraq in 2003. The question at issue was whether the ECHR applied extra-territorially to safeguard British troops abroad, in particular when serving in areas not under UK control. If jurisdiction existed under Article 1, the next question was whether the family of Smith could make a claim under Article 2 against the Ministry of Defence. A majority in the Supreme Court concluded that ECHR jurisdiction did not protect Jason Smith's rights, as he had died in an area deemed to be outside UK control.[87]

**The victim test**

Section 7(7) HRA states that "For the purposes of this section, a person is a victim of an unlawful act only if he would be a victim for the purposes of Article 34 of the Convention if proceedings were brought in the European Court of Human Rights in respect of that act."

Article 34 ECHR underlines that "The Court may receive applications from any person, nongovernmental organisation or group of individuals claiming to be the victim of a violation by one of the High Contracting Parties of the rights set forth in the Convention or the Protocols thereto. The High Contracting Parties undertake not to hinder in any way the effective exercise of this right."

Until the HRA was introduced, UK citizens had to prove that they had suffered a violation under Article 34 ECHR. In ***Klass v. Germany,*** the ECtHR interpreted 'victim' to mean directly affected.[88]

---

[85] *Al-Skeini and others v. UK*, Application no. 55721/07, 7 July 2011.
[86] R (Smith) v. Secretary of State for Defence [2010] UKSC 29.
[87] BPP, p. 110.
[88] *Klass v. Germany,* Application no. 5029/71, 6 September 1978.

Furthermore, the ECtHR has broadened its victim test by adding indirect and potential victims. If the direct victim dies before s/he can lodge an application before the ECtHR, and you are the next of kin, you can bring a claim as an indirect victim of the death or disappearance of your relative. Moreover, an alien whose removal has been ordered, but is yet to be carried out, and where this could result in inhuman or degrading treatment, or torture, in the receiving state, may bring a claim as a potential victim.[89]

Hence, since the inception of the HRA, no change has occurred since section 7(7) HRA 1998 verifies the direct, indirect/potential victim tests.

**The time limit**

Prior to the HRA, UK citizens had to bring a claim within a period of six months from the date on which the final decision was taken by the domestic courts (Article 35 ECHR).

Since the HRA was introduced, Section 7(5) HRA 1998 limits the time period for UK citizens to bring their ECHR claims to **one year**, although the court may extend this where fair.

Section 5(5) HRA states that "Proceedings under subsection (1)(a) must be brought before the end of: a) The period of one year beginning with the date on which the act complained of took place; b) Such longer period as the court or tribunal considers equitable having regard to all the circumstances."

**10. What are the key principles in human rights law?**

**Positive obligations:** Positive obligations compel State authorities to take steps to protect Convention rights. These obligations are generally not explicitly mentioned in the text but the Court has construed them.[90]

**Negative obligation:** Negative obligations mean that State authorities have to avoid acting in a manner that might infringe Convention rights. This is how most Convention rights are drawn up.[91]

It is important to underline the fact that these obligations originate from Article 1 of the Convention. This article stipulates that High Contracting Parties must ensure everyone in their jurisdiction possesses the rights and freedoms enshrined in the Convention.

---

[89] European Court of Human Rights, 'The admissibility of an application', 2015, https://www.echr.coe.int/Documents/COURtalks_Inad_Talk_ENG.PDF (accessed 30 July 2021), p. 3.
[90] Council of Europe, 'ECHR Toolkit: Some Definitions', https://www.coe.int/en/web/echr-toolkit/definitions, (accessed 30 July 2021).
[91] Ibid.

**Margin of appreciation:** It means the room for manoeuvre that the Strasbourg mechanisms allow to national authorities to use their discretionary powers, when meeting their obligations under the ECHR.[92] Naturally, this margin of appreciation varies depending on existing circumstances, the issue at hand and precedents.[93]

**Proportionality:** This is a term that describes the balancing of freedoms on the one hand and restrictions on the other hand. The principle of proportionality means there must be a reasonable relationship between an objective to be reached and the way that objective is achieved.[94] Proportionality is relevant in the category of 'qualified right', in which State authorities are legally allowed to intervene in certain situations. Before restrictions can be implemented on this freedom there are three stage tests that must be followed:

**a-)** Any State intervention must be legal (in accordance with law or prescribed by law). This includes statutes, statutory instruments, byelaws and court judgments. The legislation in question should be sufficiently precise and incorporate a provision to protect against arbitrary measures by the authorities.[95] In other words, the law in question should contain foreseeability and accessibility safeguards against arbitrariness in implementation.[96]

**b-)** One of the legitimate aims cited in Article 8(2), 9(2), 10(2) or 11(2) should be used as justification as follows: national security, territorial integrity, public safety, the economic well-being of the country, for the prevention of disorder or crime, for the protection of public order, health or morals; for the protection of the reputation, rights and freedoms of others, or for preventing the disclosure of information received in confidence, or for maintaining the authority and impartiality of the judiciary.

This is a question asked by the Court at the second stage. Since it is up to the respondent State to make clear the purpose or purposes of the interference, and the fact that reasons that may be cited for any interference are so all-encompassing – for instance, in the interests of national security – a State is usually able to construct a reasonable justification to support interference. Applicants very often claim that the justification asserted by the State is not the

---

[92] Greer, S., *The Margin of Appreciation: Interpretation and Discretion under the European Convention on Human Rights*, Council of Europe, 2000, p. 5; See also Council of Europe, 'The Margin of Appreciation', https://www.coe.int/ t/dghl/cooperation/lisbonnetwork/themis/echr/paper2_en.asp#P65_400 (accessed 30 July 2021).
[93] Kilkelly, U., The right to respect for private and family life: A guide to the implementation of Article 8 of the European Convention on Human Rights, Council of Europe, 2003, p. 32.
[94] Clayton, R. and Tomlinson, H., *The Law of Human Rights*, Oxford, 2000, p. 278; See also Council of Europe, 'The Margin of Appreciation'.
[95] Kilkelly, p. 25.
[96] *Silver and Others v. UK*, Application nos. 5947/72; 6205/73; 7052/75; 7061/75; 7107/75; 7113/75; 7136/75, 25 March 1983, para. 90.

'real' grounds for the interference at issue, but the Court has not been open to accepting such claims. On the contrary, the Court has generally not examined in detail the justifications cited by the State as the reason for its actions, often combining the aims cited – such as the protection of health and morals and the protection of the rights and freedoms of others – into one reason.[97] Hence, the Court has very rarely taken the step of rejecting the reasons given by States, and accepted that they were acting in pursuit of the stated aims. This has been the case even when the applicant may disagree.[98]

c-) It 'must be necessary in a democratic society'. This means that any intervention must 'be a pressing social need'[99], and that this intervention 'be proportionate to the legitimate aim pursued'.[100] As for a 'democratic society', it is a society based on the principles of pluralism, tolerance and open-mindedness.[101] For a State to have 'some' justification for taking the measures in question is obviously not sufficient as any interference must be 'necessary'. As regards the meaning of 'necessary', in **Handyside v. UK** the Court said that while

> ... it is not synonymous with "indispensable" ... neither has it the flexibility of such expressions as "admissible", "ordinary", "useful", "reasonable" or "desirable".[102]

National authorities are granted a margin of appreciation when it comes to the matter of pressing social need.[103] The reason for States having a margin of appreciation is on account of the fact that as some cases are very complex and sensitive, national authorities may be able to better evaluate each case in their own circumstances and ascertain the appropriate steps to take.[104]

## SAMPLE PRACTICES:

### 1. Case:

Andrew has been the victim of wrongful arrest at the hands of a police officer. He is not inclined to make a fuss about it, as he does not think it is worth it and might make things worse. However, his brother, James, is very upset about it

---

[97] *Open Door Counselling v. Ireland*, Application no. 14234/88, 29 October 1992.
[98] Kilkelly, p. 30.
[99] *Olsson v. Sweden*, Application no. 10465/83, 24 March 1988, para. 67.
[100] *Coster v. UK*, Application no. 24876/94, 18 January 2001, para. 104; *Jane Smith v. UK [GC]*, Application no. 25154/94, 18 January 2001, para. 54.
[101] *Handyside v. UK*, Application no. 5493/72, 07 December 1976, para. 49.
[102] Ibid, para. 48.
[103] Ibid, para. 11.
[104] *Olsson v. Sweden (No. 2)*, Application no. 13441/87, 30 October 1992, para. 91.

and is determined to take action against the local police force under the HRA 1998 in order to gain redress for his brother.

**Is it possible for James to do this?**

- Section 7(1) of the HRA 1998: "a person who claims that a public authority has acted in a way which is made unlawful [by section 6(1)] may …bring proceedings … but only if he is a victim of an unlawful act…"
- Section 7(7) of the HRA 1998: "For the purposes of this section, a person is a victim of an unlawful act only if he would be a victim for the purposes of Article 34 of the Convention if proceedings were brought in the European Court of Human Rights in respect of that act."
- Article 34 of the ECHR: "The Court may receive applications from any person, nongovernmental organisation or group of individuals claiming to be the victim of a violation by one of the High Contracting Parties of the rights set forth in the Convention or the Protocols thereto…"

In *Klass v. Germany* a victim is described as a person who has been **directly affected** by the violation of a Convention right.

Therefore, it is evident that James will be unable to lodge a HRA claim for Andrew as he was not directly affected. In addition, he is neither an indirect nor potential victim.

## 2. Case:

Vladimir, a Russian national resident in England, had a similar experience.

**Would it be possible for him to make a HRA claim? If so, is there a time limit for making a claim of this kind in court?**

Regarding the protection of rights, nationality is not relevant.

Article 1 of the ECHR states: "The High Contracting Parties shall secure to everyone within their jurisdiction the rights and freedoms defined in Section 1 of this Convention."

Hence, a citizen of any country may lodge a claim under the HRA 1998 if they believe a public authority has breached a right safeguarded by the Convention.

**Vladimir would thus have a year to lodge a claim, according to Section 7(5) of the HRA 1998.**

## 3. Case:

James was a British soldier who suffered a fatal injury caused by a roadside bomb in Helmand Province in Afghanistan. It subsequently emerged that his wounds were made worse by a faulty protective helmet.

### Could James's parents lodge a HRA 1998 claim in connection with this incident?

In this case there is a question of the scope of jurisdiction of the HRA 1998. Generally, jurisdiction concerns the territory of the State in question, as per Article 1 of the ECHR.

However, HRA 1998 can have extra-territorial application. Based on the cases of ***Al-Skeini and Others v. UK*** and ***R (Smith) 2010***, James's parents would, as his next of kin, have the right to make a claim under the HRA.

## 4. Case:

Section 6(1) of the HRA mentions the obligation for "public authorities" to act in a manner that is compatible with Convention rights.

### Which of the following bodies would be considered core public authorities?

- **(i)   The Home Office.**
- **(ii)   The police**
- **(iii)   Sainsbury's**
- **(iv)   Liverpool City Council**

There are two types of 'public authority': **a-) 'Core'** public authorities, bodies which on account of their function are clearly public authorities, and **b-) 'Hybrid'** public authorities, concerns like privatised utility companies, that do not seem to meet the criteria of a public authority, but carry out public functions.

This distinction between the two types of authority is significant as it seems that while 'core' public authorities have to meet the Section 6(1) obligation regarding all their functions, a 'hybrid' public authority only has this obligation as regards acts which are of a public character.

It is obvious that **(i), (ii) and (iv) are all core public authorities,** with an obligation under Section 6(1) for all their acts. They are public authorities that carry out core functions as an adjunct of the State.

# CHAPTER V

# FUNDAMENTAL FREEDOMS IN THE HUMAN RIGHTS ACT/EUROPEAN CONVENTION ON HUMAN RIGHTS

**Learning Outcomes:**

In this chapter, you should be able to understand:

- ✓ the scope of Articles 2, 3, 4, 5, 6, 7, 8, 9, 10, 11, 12, 14 and 15;
- ✓ the fundamental rights in the Police and Criminal Evidence Act (PACE) 1984.

**Questions and Answers:**

**1. What is the scope of Article 2?**

Article 2 states that

1. Everyone's right to life shall be protected by law. No one shall be deprived of his life intentionally save in the execution of a sentence of a court following his conviction of a crime for which this penalty is provided by law.

2. Deprivation of life shall not be regarded as inflicted in contravention of this Article when it results from the use of force which is no more than absolutely necessary:

(a) in defence of any person from unlawful violence;

(b) in order to effect a lawful arrest or to prevent the escape of a person lawfully detained;

(c) in action lawfully taken for the purpose of quelling a riot or insurrection.

The right to life is the first right in the ECHR since it is the most fundamental human right of all.[105] As the Court underlined in its Grand Chamber (GC) judgment in the case of ***McCann and others v. UK***:

Article 2 ranks as one of the most fundamental provisions in the Convention – indeed one which, in peacetime, admits of no derogation

---

[105] Korff, D., *The Right to Life: A Guide to the Implementation of Article 2 of the European Convention on Human Rights*, Council of Europe, 2006, p. 6

under Article 15. Together with Article 3 of the Convention [the prohibition of torture], it also enshrines one of the basic values of the democratic societies making up the Council of Europe.[106]

The second sentence in Article 2 (1) applies to the death penalty, which in times of peace has either been abrogated (Protocol No. 6) or entirely annulled (Protocol No. 13) for the State Parties that have signed up to these protocols.[107]

There is an important obligation on the State to investigate the circumstances of deaths – particularly those involving State agents – effectively. This is the so-called 'procedural' obligation established by the ECtHR in the ***Gül v. Turkey*** case.[108]

## 2. What is the scope of Article 3?

Article 3 states that

> No one shall be subjected to torture or to inhuman or degrading treatment or punishment.

Article 3 covers many different kinds of assault, involving both physical integrity and those on an individual's dignity. The case-law and the way the Convention is implemented provides it with its lifeblood, and a study of that case-law demonstrates how extensive the prohibition in Article 3 is, and how it should be applied. The broad extent of cases reveals several issues regarding the scope of Article 3 such as:

- First of all, a broad range of types of behaviour, in addition to specific acts, are banned under Article 3.
- Possible perpetrators of Article 3 contraventions are also diverse.
- Both objective and subjective tests are used to determine whether certain behaviour or deeds breach Article 3.
- Article 3 has both substantive and procedural aspects, including an obligation to look into prima facie allegations of torture and other inhuman treatment.
- Article 3 can be breached by both deliberate ill-treatment and also by negligence or failure to act, or ensure proper care is provided.
- Article 3 contains both negative and positive obligations meaning that certain actions should be avoided (negative obligation), and that

---

[106] *McCann and others v. UK* [GC], Application no. 18984/91, 5 September 1995, para. 147; See also *Soering v. UK*, Application no. 14038/88, 7 July 1989, para 88.
[107] Korff, p. 6.
[108] *Gül v. Turkey,* Application no. 4870/02, 8 June 2010.

positive steps should be taken to ensure individuals' rights are protected from treatment that is prohibited (positive obligation).[109]

## 3. What is the scope of Article 4?

Article 4 states that

1. No one shall be held in slavery or servitude.

2. No one shall be required to perform forced or compulsory labour.

3. For the purpose of this Article the term "forced or compulsory labour" shall not include:

   a. any work required to be done in the ordinary course of detention imposed according to the provisions of Article 5 of this Convention or during conditional release from such detention;

   b. any service of a military character or, in case of conscientious objectors in countries where they are recognised, service exacted instead of compulsory military service;

   c. any service exacted in case of an emergency or calamity threatening the life or well-being of the community;

   d. any work or service which forms part of normal civic obligations.

Article 4(1) of the Convention states "no one shall be held in slavery or servitude". Differing from most of the substantive sections of the Convention, Article 4(1) permits no exceptions and no derogation from it is possible under Article 15(2), even if a public emergency threatens the country *(C.N. v. UK, para. 65; Stummer v. Austria [GC], para. 116)*.

Article 4(2) of the Convention bans forced or compulsory labour. The term 'forced or compulsory labour' has the purpose of safeguarding against serious exploitation, such as forced prostitution, regardless of whether it is related to a particular human trafficking context. Any such behaviour might be deemed 'slavery' or 'servitude' under Article 4, or involve another provision of the Convention *(S.M. v. Croatia [GC], paras. 300 and 303)*.

Article 4(3) of the Convention is not meant to restrict the exercise of the right enshrined in paragraph 2, but to determine the boundaries of that right, as it comprises a whole with paragraph 2 and sets down what the term 'forced or

---

[109] Reidy, A., *The Prohibition of Torture: A guide to the implementation of Article 3 of the European Convention on Human Rights*, Council of Europe, 2002, p. 9.

compulsory labour' does not incorporate *(Stummer v. Austria [GC], para. 120).*[110]

## 4. What is the scope of Article 5?

Article 5 states that

1. Everyone has the right to liberty and security of person. No one shall be deprived of his liberty save in the following cases and in accordance with a procedure prescribed by law:

   a) the lawful detention of a person after conviction by a competent court;

   b) the lawful arrest or detention of a person for noncompliance with the lawful order of a court or in order to secure the fulfilment of any obligation prescribed by law;

   c) the lawful arrest or detention of a person effected for the purpose of bringing him before the competent legal authority on reasonable suspicion of having committed an offence or when it is reasonably considered necessary to prevent his committing an offence or fleeing after having done so;

   d) the detention of a minor by lawful order for the purpose of educational supervision or his lawful detention for the purpose of bringing him before the competent legal authority;

   e) the lawful detention of persons for the prevention of the spreading of infectious diseases, of persons of unsound mind, alcoholics or drug addicts or vagrants;

   f) the lawful arrest or detention of a person to prevent his effecting an unauthorised entry into the country or of a person against whom action is being taken with a view to deportation or extradition.

2. Everyone who is arrested shall be informed promptly, in a language which he understands, of the reasons for his arrest and of any charge against him.

3. Everyone arrested or detained in accordance with the provisions of paragraph 1 (c) of this Article shall be brought promptly before a judge or other officer authorised by law to exercise judicial power and shall be entitled to trial within a reasonable time or to release pending trial. Release may be conditioned by guarantees to appear for trial.

---

[110] European Court of Human Rights, 'Guide on Article 4 of the European Convention on Human Rights', 30 April 2021, https://www.echr.coe.int/documents/guide_art_4_eng.pdf (accessed 30 July 2021), p. 5.

4. Everyone who is deprived of his liberty by arrest or detention shall be entitled to take proceedings by which the lawfulness of his detention shall be decided speedily by a court and his release ordered if the detention is not lawful.

5. Everyone who has been the victim of arrest or detention in contravention of the provisions of this Article shall have an enforceable right to compensation.

In addition, the right to liberty is safeguarded in Article 1 of Protocol No. 4 as follows:

No one shall be deprived of his liberty merely on the ground of inability to fulfil a contractual obligation.

The right to liberty is an absolutely basic right, which all individuals should be able to possess. To be deprived of this right will probably directly affect the enjoyment of many other rights, including the right to family and private life, the right to freedom of assembly, association and expression and the right to freedom of movement.[111] The ECtHR has emphasised the significance of this right in many cases. In **Kurt v. Turkey**, the Court concluded:

…that the authors of the Convention reinforced the individual's protection against arbitrary deprivation of his or her liberty by guaranteeing a corpus of substantive rights which are intended to minimise the risks of arbitrariness by allowing the act of deprivation of liberty to be amenable to independent judicial scrutiny and by securing the accountability of the authorities for that act. […] What is at stake is both the protection of the physical liberty of individuals as well as their personal security in a context which, in the absence of safeguards, could result in a subversion of the rule of law and place detainees beyond the reach of the most rudimentary forms of legal protection.[112]

Article 5 addresses the physical liberty of the individual; the aim of this article is to prevent anyone being deprived of that freedom arbitrarily. It does not deal with simple restrictions on freedom of movement, which are dealt with in Article 2 of Protocol No. 4. The difference is one of intensity, not substance; between limits on movement serious enough to come under deprivation of liberty in Article 5(1) and minor restrictions of liberty which fall under Article 2 of Protocol No. 4.

---

[111] Macovei, M., *The Right to Liberty and Security of the Person: A guide to the implementation of Article 5 of the European Convention on Human Rights*, Council of Europe, 2002, pp. 5-6
[112] *Kurt v. Turkey*, Application no. 24276/94, 25 May 1998, para. 123.

It is also important to note that the term deprivation of liberty is not limited to the traditional detention after an arrest or conviction, but may occur in other different forms.[113]

## 5. What is the scope of Article 6?

Article 6 states that

1. In the determination of his civil rights and obligations or of any criminal charge against him, everyone is entitled to a fair and public hearing within a reasonable time by an independent and impartial tribunal established by law. Judgment shall be pronounced publicly but the press and public may be excluded from all or part of the trial in the interests of morals, public order or national security in a democratic society, where the interests of juveniles or the protection of the private life of the parties so require, or to the extent strictly necessary in the opinion of the court in special circumstances where publicity would prejudice the interests of justice.

2. Everyone charged with a criminal offence shall be presumed innocent until proved guilty according to law.

3. Everyone charged with a criminal offence has the following minimum rights:

   a) to be informed promptly, in a language which he understands and in detail, of the nature and cause of the accusation against him;

   b) to have adequate time and facilities for the preparation of his defence;

   c) to defend himself in person or through legal assistance of his own choosing or, if he has not sufficient means to pay for legal assistance, to be given it free when the interests of justice so require;

   d) to examine or have examined witnesses against him and to obtain the attendance and examination of witnesses on his behalf under the same conditions as witnesses against him; to

   e) have the free assistance of an interpreter if he cannot understand or speak the language used in court.

Article 6 ensures that an individual has the right to a fair and public hearing in which his civil rights and obligations regarding any criminal charge against him are protected. In the case of ***Delcourt v. Belgium***, the Court stated that

---

[113] European Court of Human Rights, 'Guide on Article 5 of the European Convention on Human Rights', 30 April 2021, https://www.echr.coe.int/documents/guide_art_5_eng.pdf (accessed 30 July 2021), p. 8.

In a democratic society within the meaning of the Convention, the right to a fair administration of justice holds such a prominent place that a restrictive interpretation of Article 6 (1) would not correspond to the aim and the purpose of that provision.[114]

The first paragraph of Article 6 is applicable in both civil and criminal cases, but the second and third paragraphs only refer to criminal cases. Nevertheless, safeguards similar to those in Article 6 (2) and 6 (3) may also apply in civil cases under certain conditions.

The State has a positive responsibility to do everything needed to see that these rights are protected and implemented. This obligation also involves systems of justice being provided with sufficient financial resources to carry out their duties.[115]

## 6. What is the scope of Article 7?

Article 7 states that

1. No one shall be held guilty of any criminal offence on account of any act or omission which did not constitute a criminal offence under national or international law at the time when it was committed. Nor shall a heavier penalty be imposed than the one that was applicable at the time the criminal offence was committed.

2. This Article shall not prejudice the trial and punishment of any person for any act or omission which, at the time when it was committed, was criminal according to the general principles of law recognised by civilised nations.

The safeguards in Article 7, which are crucial elements of the rule of law, have a key place in the Convention system of protection, which is indicated by the fact that States cannot derogate from it under Article 15, even in the event of war or another public emergency. These measures must be applied in a manner that ensures there are sufficient safeguards in place to prevent arbitrary prosecution, conviction and punishment *(S. W. v. UK, para. 34; C.R. v. UK, para. 32)*.[116]

Article 7 not only bans the retrospective use of criminal law to the detriment of a person accused of an offence. It also encapsulates the tenets that make clear only the law can determine a crime and set out a penalty and that the

---

[114] *Delcourt v. Belgium*, Application no. 2689/65, 17 January 1970, para. 25.
[115] Mole, N. and Harby, C., *The right to a fair trial: A guide to the implementation of Article 6 of the European Convention on Human Rights*, Council of Europe, 2006, pp. 5-8.
[116] *S.W. v. UK*, Application no. 20166/92, 22 November 1995, para. 34; *C.R. v. UK*, Application no. 20190/92, 22 November 1995, para. 32.

criminal law must not be broadly interpreted to harm, perhaps by analogy, the rights of an accused person *(Kokkinakis v. Greece, para. 52)*.[117]

Article 7 is only applicable when an individual has been 'found guilty' of committing a criminal offence. It cannot be applied in ongoing prosecutions, for instance *(Lukanov v. Bulgaria)*, or in extradition cases *(X v. the Netherlands)*.[118] For the Convention, there is no 'conviction' until it has been legally ascertained that an offence has occurred.[119]

## 7. What is the scope of Article 8?

Article 8 states that

1. Everyone has the right to respect for his private and family life, his home and his correspondence.

2. There shall be no interference by a public authority with the exercise of this right except such as is in accordance with the law and is necessary in a democratic society in the interests of national security, public safety or the economic well-being of the country, for the prevention of disorder or crime, for the protection of health or morals, or for the protection of the rights and freedoms of others.

Article 8 has two parts. Article 8 paragraph 1 lays down the rights which the State shall protect for an individual: the right to respect for private life, family life, home and correspondence. The second part, Article 8 paragraph 2, establishes that these rights are not absolute, since public authorities may interfere in certain circumstances. Article 8 paragraph 2 also sets out what the circumstances are in which public authorities my interfere with these rights in Article 8 paragraph 1; solely lawful State interference deemed necessary in a democratic society in line with one or more of the legitimate aims in Article 8 paragraph 2 will be considered an acceptable limitation of a person's Article 8 rights.[120]

## 8. What is the scope of Article 9?

Article 9 states that

1. Everyone has the right to freedom of thought, conscience and religion; this right includes freedom to change his religion or belief and freedom, either alone or in community with others and in public or private, to

---

[117] *Kokkinakis v. Greece,* Application no. 14307/88, 25 May 1993, para. 52.
[118] *Lukanov v. Bulgaria,* Commission decision, Application no. 21915/93, 12 January 1995; *X v. the Netherlands,* Commission decision, Application no. 7512/76, 6 July 1976.
[119] European Court of Human Rights, 'Guide on Article 7 of the European Convention on Human Rights', 30 April 2021, https://www.echr.coe.int/Documents/Guide_Art_7_ENG.pdf, pp. 5-6
[120] Kilkelly, p. 6.

manifest his religion or belief, in worship, teaching, practice and observance.

2. Freedom to manifest one's religion or beliefs shall be subject only to such limitations as are prescribed by law and are necessary in a democratic society in the interests of public safety, for the protection of public order, health or morals, or for the protection of the rights and freedoms of others.

Furthermore, Article 2 of Protocol No. 1 to the Convention addresses one facet of freedom of religion, the right of parents to have their children educated in a manner that complies with their religious beliefs:

No person shall be denied the right to education. In the exercise of any functions which it assumes in relation to education and to teaching, the State shall respect the right of parents to ensure such education and teaching for their children in conformity with their own religious and philosophical convictions.

Freedom of thought, conscience and religion is one of the cornerstones of a 'democratic society' as set down in the Convention. The religious aspect of this freedom is not only a key element in the identity of believers and how they perceive life, but is also very important for atheists, agnostics, sceptics and the unconcerned.[121]

The first sentence in the first paragraph, up to the semicolon, protects absolutely the right to freedom of thought, conscience and religion for all. This is the *forum internum* (internal aspect) of this freedom, that no individual or State can interfere with. The *forum externum* (external aspect) of this freedom involves the manifesting of religion or belief, in worship, teaching, practice and observance. The second paragraph emphasises that this right is not absolute and that public authorities may introduce limitations to Article 9 in certain circumstances.[122] Any such limitations must be necessary in a democratic society and be proportional.

## 9. What is the scope of Article 10?

Article 10 states that

1. Everyone has the right to freedom of expression. This right shall include freedom to hold opinions and to receive and impart information and ideas without interference by public authority and regardless of frontiers.

---

[121] European Court of Human Rights, 'Guide on Article 9 of the European Convention on Human Rights', 30 April 2021, https://www.echr.coe.int/Documents/Guide_Art_9_ENG.pdf, p. 8.
[122] Murdoch, J., *Freedom of thought, conscience and religion: A guide to the implementation of Article 9 of the European Convention on Human Rights*, Council of Europe, 2007, pp 10-11.

This Article shall not prevent States from requiring the licensing of broadcasting, television or cinema enterprises.

2. The exercise of these freedoms, since it carries with it duties and responsibilities, may be subject to such formalities, conditions, restrictions or penalties as are prescribed by law and are necessary in a democratic society, in the interests of national security, territorial integrity or public safety, for the prevention of disorder or crime, for the protection of health or morals, for the protection of the reputation or rights of others, for preventing the disclosure of information received in confidence, or for maintaining the authority and impartiality of the judiciary.

Freedom of expression is itself a right, besides being part of other rights safeguarded by the Convention, like freedom of assembly. However, freedom of expression can also clash with other rights protected by the Convention, such as the right to a fair trial, to respect for private life, to freedom of thought, conscience and religion. In the event of such a clash occurring, the Court endeavours to find equilibrium and establish the primacy of one right over the other. This balancing of interests takes into account the importance of the two rights in question.[123]

The Court has stressed the importance of this Article several times, it being relevant not only to 'information' or 'ideas' that are welcomed or regarded as inoffensive, but also to those considered offensive, shocking or disturbing. Key attributes of pluralism are tolerance and broadmindedness, essential aspects of a 'democratic society' *(Handyside v. UK, para. 49; Observer and Guardian v. UK, para. 59).*[124]

States are expected as part of their positive obligations to introduce an effective mechanism to protect authors and journalists so that public debate may take place, with everyone able to voice their opinions and ideas without fear. This is particularly true if these opinions diverge from those advocated by the authorities or by a large proportion of public opinion, or if they cause shock or outrage in society *(Dink v. Turkey, para. 137).*[125] Hence, Article 10 of the

---

[123] Macovei, M., *Freedom of Expression: A guide to the implementation of Article 10 of the European Convention on Human Rights*, Council of Europe, 2004, p. 6.

[124] *Handyside v. UK*, Application no. 5493/72, 7 December 1976, Series A no. 24, para. 49; *Observer and Guardian v. UK*, Application no. 13585/88, 26 November 1991, Series A no. 216, para. 59.

[125] *Dink v. Turkey*, Application nos. 2668/07, 6102/08, 30079/08, 14 September 2010, para. 137.

Convention has a very broad scope, both as regards the substance of the ideas and opinions aired, and the form in which this is done.[126]

The right to freedom of expression is not an absolute right; it may be restricted in line with paragraph 2 of Article 10, like Articles 8 and 9.

## 10. What is the scope of Article 11?

Article 11 states that

1.  Everyone has the right to freedom of peaceful assembly and to freedom of association with others, including the right to form and to join trade unions for the protection of his interests.

2.  No restrictions shall be placed on the exercise of these rights other than such as are prescribed by law and are necessary in a democratic society in the interests of national security or public safety, for the prevention of disorder or crime, for the protection of health or morals or for the protection of the rights and freedoms of others. This Article shall not prevent the imposition of lawful restrictions on the exercise of these rights by members of the armed forces, of the police or of the administration of the State.

The concept of 'assembly' in this Article is an autonomous one. It deals with gatherings that are not subject to domestic legal regulation, regardless of whether notification or authorisation is needed or whether they are exempt. Hence, the Court found Article 11 applied to a peaceful 'walkabout' when groups of individuals came together purposefully to voice a political message. The applicant in this case did not regard the gathering as 'marches' or 'meetings' requiring notification according to domestic law *(Navalnyy v. Russia [GC], para. 106)*. This right governs both meetings of a private nature and gatherings in public places, static or a procession. Moreover, this right can be exercised by individual participants and by organisers of gatherings *(Kudrevičius and Others v. Lithuania [GC], para. 91)*.[127]

The right to freedom of assembly also includes the right to choose how, when and where the gathering will take place, within the boundaries outlined in paragraph 2 of Article 11 *(Sáska v. Hungary, para. 21)*. Hence, if the assembly site is important for the participants, an order moving it elsewhere may constitute a violation of their freedom of assembly under Article 11 of the

---

[126] European Court of Human Rights, 'Guide on Article 10 of the European Convention on Human Rights', 30 December 2020, https://www.echr.coe.int/Documents/Guide_Art_10_ENG.pdf (accessed 30 July 2021), pp.11-12.

[127] *Navalnyy v. Russia [GC]*, Application nos. 29580/12 and 4 others, 15 November 2018, para. 106; *Kudrevičius and Others v. Lithuania [GC]*, Application no. 37553/05, ECHR 2015, para. 91.

Convention *(The United Macedonian Organisation Ilinden and Ivanov v. Bulgaria, para. 103)*.[128]

Article 11 of the Convention only safeguards the right to 'peaceful assembly', but does not protect the freedom to hold a violent demonstration. The provisions of Article 11 hence are valid for all gatherings except where the organisers and participants intend to incite violence or otherwise threaten the principles of a democratic society *(Kudrevičius and Others v. Lithuania [GC], para. 92)*.[129]

This right is also not absolute. It, too, is subject to restrictions in line with paragraph 2 of Article 11, just like Articles 8, 9 and 10.

## 11. What is the scope of Article 12?

Article 12 states that

> Men and women of marriageable age have the right to marry and to found a family, according to the national laws governing the exercise of this right.

The wording of Article 12 of the Convention is quite narrow and the Court's and the former European Commission of Human Rights' interpretation of it has not expanded its scope significantly. Article 12 does not apply to family life apart from marriage and having a family. Furthermore, the right to found a family without marriage is not mentioned in Article 12.

Moreover, exercise of the right safeguarded under Article 12 is subject to domestic provisions. Unlike Article 8, which mentions the 'right to respect for private and family life', very similar in meaning 'to marry and to found a family', Article 12 does not allow any grounds for State interference such as that permitted under paragraph 2 of Article 8 ('in accordance with the law' and 'necessary in a democratic society', for reasons such as 'the protection of health or morals' or 'the protection of the rights and freedoms of others'). Therefore, when dealing with a case under Article 12, the Court does not implement the tests of 'necessity' or 'pressing social need', as it does with Article 8, instead having to decide whether the interference in question was arbitrary or

---

[128] *Sáska v. Hungary*, Application no. 58050/08, 27 November 2012, *para. 21; The United Macedonian Organisation Ilinden and Ivanov v. Bulgaria*, Application no. 44079/98, 20 October 2005, para. 103.
[129] *Kudrevičius and Others v. Lithuania [GC]*, Application no. 37553/05, 15 October 2015, para. 92; See also European Court of Human Rights, 'Guide on Article 11 of the European Convention on Human Rights', 30 April 2021, https://www.echr.coe.int/Documents/Guide_Art_11_ENG.pdf (accessed 30 July 2021), pp. 8-13.

disproportionate, with regard to the State's margin of appreciation *(Frasik v. Poland, para. 90)*.[130]

## 12. What is the scope of Article 14?

Article 14 states that

> The enjoyment of the rights and freedoms set forth in this Convention shall be secured without discrimination on any ground such as sex, race, colour, language, religion, political or other opinion, national or social origin, association with a national minority, property, birth or other status.

Article 14 of the Convention protects "the enjoyment of the rights and freedoms set out in the Convention" without being discriminated against. It is important to remember that the Court always examines Article 14 in conjunction with another provision of the Convention *(Molla Sali v. Greece [GC], para. 123)*.[131]

Furthermore, the Court has applied the provisions of Article 14 in many areas, such as:

- Employment;
- Membership of a trade union;
- Social security;
- Education;
- Right to respect for home;
- Access to justice;
- Inheritance rights;
- Access to children;
- Paternity;
- Freedom of expression, assembly and association;
- Right to an effective investigation;
- Eligibility for release on parole;
- Eligibility for tax relief.[132]

---

[130] European Court of Human Rights, 'Guide on Article 12 of the European Convention on Human Rights', 31 December 2020, https://www.echr.coe.int/Documents/Guide_Art_12_ENG.pdf (accessed 30 July 2021), p. 5.

[131] *Molla Sali v. Greece [GC]*, Application no. 20452/14, 19 December 2018, para. 123.

[132] European Court of Human Rights, 'Guide on Article 14 of the European Convention on Human Rights and on Article 1 of Protocol No. 12 to the Convention', https://www.echr.coe.int/Documents/Guide_Art_14_Art_1_Protocol_12_ENG.pdf (accessed 30 July 2021), pp. 6-7.

### 13. What is the scope of Article 15?

Article 15 states that

1. In time of war or other public emergency threatening the life of the nation any High Contracting Party may take measures derogating from its obligations under this Convention to the extent strictly required by the exigencies of the situation, provided that such measures are not inconsistent with its other obligations under international law.

2. No derogation from Article 2, except in respect of deaths resulting from lawful acts of war, or from Articles 3, 4 (paragraph 1) and 7 shall be made under this provision.

3. Any High Contracting Party availing itself of this right of derogation shall keep the Secretary General of the Council of Europe fully informed of the measures which it has taken and the reasons therefor. It shall also inform the Secretary General of the Council of Europe when such measures have ceased to operate and the provisions of the Convention are again being fully executed.

Article 15 is a clause that provides grounds for derogation. It allows Contracting States, in exceptional circumstances, to derogate, in a restricted and controlled manner, from their obligations to safeguard certain rights and freedoms under the Convention.

Article 15 has three parts. Article 15(1) outlines the conditions under which Contracting States are permitted to derogate from their obligations under the Convention. It also restricts what measures may be taken during any derogation. Article 15(2) prevents derogation from certain fundamental rights in the Convention. Article 15(3) lays down the procedural steps for a State to follow when availing itself of the right of derogation.[133]

### 14. What are the fundamental rights in the PACE 1984?

In the UK, when an individual is arrested on the suspicion that they have committed an offence, it is the usual practice for them to be taken to a police station. There, a custody officer will weigh up the evidence to determine whether it is enough to charge the person who has been arrested with the offence. According to PACE 1984, in the event that the custody officer reaches the conclusion that there is not enough evidence to charge the person, s/he has to be released. The only exception to this rule is if the officer has a justifiable

---

[133] European Court of Human Rights, 'Guide on Article 15 of the European Convention on Human Rights', 30 April 2021, https://www.echr.coe.int/documents/Guide_Art_15_ENG.pdf (accessed 30 July 2021), p. 5.

belief that the suspect needs to be detained without charge in order to secure or preserve evidence or to obtain evidence through questioning. The longest a person can be held without charge is 24 hours from the relevant time. The interpretation of 'relevant time' in PACE 1984 usually signifies the time an arrested individual arrives at the first police station. An extension of the period of detention without charge may be made for up to 36 hours from the relevant time, as long as the conditions imposed by PACE 1984 are met. A further extension is only possible under PACE 1984 if a magistrates' court issues a warrant to extend detention. The relevant procedure and conditions are laid down in PACE 1984. Please also note that the maximum total time of detention without charge must not exceed 96 hours from the relevant time.[134]

Furthermore, a suspect's access to a solicitor can be limited according to the terms of Schedule 8 of Terrorism Act 2000 and Code H of PACE for up to 48 hours. Additionally, it is worth noting that an officer of at least the rank of superintendent may prevent a suspect consulting a solicitor for up to 36 hours, as long as the conditions laid down in Code C are met, according to PACE, Section 58(6).[135]

**SAMPLE PRACTICES:**

- The police have been monitoring Leyanda for several months. They believe she intends to assassinate General Marcos with a bomb. They fire a warning shot and her hand makes a move towards her jacket. She is then shot dead. Subsequently, despite her family conducting a campaign, the police refuse to carry out a full investigation.

**Advise her mother whether there have been any violations of Article 2.**

Article 2 places a duty on the State to avoid the taking of human life except when it is absolutely necessary (Article 2(2)) and also establishes a positive obligation to take all measures possible to protect life.

However, through Convention case law the principle has been entrenched that the State has a secondary important obligation to investigate the how deaths occurred – particularly in cases involving State operatives – effectively. This is the 'procedural' obligation created by the ECtHR in the ***Gül v. Turkey*** case.

---

[134] Lexis, 'Arrest and detention—overview: Police powers of arrest without warrant', https://www.lexisnexis.com/uk/lexispsl/corporatecrime/document/391421/55KB-9471-F188-N193-00000-00/Arrest_and_detention_overview (accessed 30 July 2021).
[135] Clements, pp. 138-160.

In the case of **R (Amin) v SS Home Dept 2003** – involving the murder of a young Asian man in Feltham YOI by a racist in the same cell – the HoL stipulated that an 'effective investigation' had to at a minimum be public, independent and include the full participation of the family. Complete reasons for any decision should also be required.[136]

In Leyanda's case, the court may deem it necessary for any investigation to examine systemic failings of the system. This would include exploring whether the police had been trained correctly and questions asked about the intelligence. Hence, in sum, the behaviour of the police would probably be castigated, both for the way they acted and, particularly, for their rebuffing of calls to carry out a subsequent investigation. Therefore, **it is likely to be a violation of Article 2**.

- Andrew is held custody by the police. During this time his clothing was removed and twice an iron bar was used to strike the soles of his feet.

**Advise Andrew whether there have been any violations of Article 3.**

Article 3 bans 'torture or inhuman or degrading treatment or punishment'. In **Ireland v. UK** (pertaining to the self-styled 'Five Techniques' of interrogation the UK security services in Northern Ireland employed in the 70s), the Court construed 'torture' as acts inflicting "particular intensity and cruelty … intense physical and mental suffering". In cases dealt with the victim's gender, age and health will be considered. **It is not likely that what happened to Andrew will be deemed 'torture'**, as the ECtHR did not conclude that 'torture' had taken place in the **Ireland** case.[137]

However, the term 'degrading' was viewed as something that could produce 'feelings of fear, anguish and inferiority, capable of humiliating and debasing' a person. A person having his clothes forcibly removed in front of other people and being struck with a heavy object would seem to meet the criterion of degrading treatment. In the **Pretty v. UK**, the Court stated treatment of this kind could break a person's moral and physical resistance.[138] Hence, **it is likely that what happened to Andrew will be deemed 'degrading treatment'**.

---

[136] R (Amin) v. SS Home Dept [2003] UKHL 51.
[137] *Ireland v. UK*, Application no. 5310/71, 20 March 2018.
[138] *Pretty v. UK*, Application no. 2346/02, 29 April 2002.

- On 20 January 2015, the pharmacy at London Community Hospital is broken into in the evening and four men leave, taking with them a large quantity of prescription drugs. The next morning at 8 am two police officers go to Max's apartment and arrest him under section 30 of the (fictitious) Hospital Drugs Act 2005 ("the Act") (the HDA) which states: 'A police officer may arrest any person on reasonable suspicion of theft of drugs or other medication intended for medical use in hospitals or clinics.'

Max is taken to London Police Station and interviewed under caution. Firstly, he is asked a about where he was the previous evening. He asks why and what they think he has done, and one of the officers, a PC Mark, replies: "Don't worry about the details. We know it was you; it's typical of you, and we've got proof that one of them was at least 6 foot 4, just like you."

Max is held in custody from the time of his arrest (8 am on 21 January to around 9.30 pm on 22 January = at least 37 and a half hours).

**Advise Max whether there have been any violations of Article 5.**

Article 5 stipulates that the police must have reasonable suspicion – Article 5(1)(c) – and that any action taken is in line with a procedure (prescribed by law).

The arrest is laid down in Section 30 of the HDA which complies with Article 5(1)(c) in requiring reasonable suspicion *(Sunday Times v. UK* and *Gillan and Quinton v. UK)*.[139]

However, it is apparent that there was no way the police could have had reasonable suspicion when Max was arrested – their only justification was that Max had a record (for an un-related offence) and he is very tall.

In the case of *Fox, Campbell and Hartley v. UK*, the ECtHR stated that reasonable suspicion means objective evidence.[140]

Hence, a breach of Article 5(1)(c) appears to have occurred.

**Concerning Max's detention by the police,** Article 5(3) applies here. In the UK, the Terrorism Act 2006 permits fourteen days detention but only if a judge is notified after the first 48 hours. Furthermore, PACE states detention shall be no more than 36 hours (on police authority only and detention exceeding

---

[139] *Sunday Times v. UK,* Application no. 6538/74, 26 April 1979; *Gillan and Quinton v. UK,* Application no 4158/05, 12 January 2010.
[140] *Fox, Campbell and Hartley v. UK,* Application nos. 2244/86; 12245/86; 12383/86, 27 March 1991.

24 hours requires approval by a senior officer, superintendent or higher – Section 42(1) *(Brogan v. UK)*.[141]

**Max's detention therefore seems excessive, but it is a debatable matter.**

- Tgovia is an island country in a strategically important region and an ally of the UK. It has a bad record when it comes to human rights and its President, General Marcos, is coming to the UK for an official visit. To avoid General Marcos suffering any embarrassment during his visit, the (fictitious) Tgovia (Good Relations Act) Act ('the Act') is passed in Parliament.

- Alex is arrested on the basis of section 8 of the Act and detained for in custody for 72 hours. Despite Alex making many requests to see his solicitor while in custody, he is denied access because the police think the solicitor will advise him to remain silent. Consequently, Alex confesses and he is charged under section 7 of the Act.

**Advise Alex whether there have been any violations of Article 6.**

**The first question to answer is whether Article 6 is applicable:**

Yes, it is because Alex has been charged with a criminal offence.

Note that Article 6 applies as long as the suspects are charged. If they are merely interrogated and then released without charge, Article 6 is not applicable.

**Secondly, the question of being denied access to a solicitor will be explored:**

Article 6(3)(c) states that a person charged with a criminal offence can defend themselves through legal assistance which they choose, or be granted legal assistance if they are unable to pay for it (when the interests of justice demand it).

*John Murray v. UK* indicates that if a person is denied access to legal advice when questioned after arrest (and not only after being charged) this could constitute a violation of Article 6, since this puts a suspect at a disadvantage in that his rights throughout the legal process could be affected (In the *Murray* case he did not see a solicitor for 48 hours because a detective superintendent thought that this would threaten the general investigation into a terrorism-related incident in Northern Ireland).

In a similar case, that of *Magee v. UK*, Gerard Magee was detained under section 12 of the Prevention of Terrorism Act 1984 regarding an attempted

---

[141] *Brogan v. UK,* [1988] 11 EHRR 117.

bomb attack on soldiers. He was also denied access to a solicitor for two days and questioned constantly by teams of detectives regarding his role in a bombing incident. He admitted to being involved during the sixth interview and subsequently signed a long confession statement.

The ECtHR mentioned the fact that the applicant had specifically asked to see a solicitor when he arrived at Castlereagh Police Office. After the decision was taken to deny the applicant access to a solicitor, he was kept in isolation. The ECtHR's opinion was that the conditions under which the applicant was held and his isolation were deliberately psychologically coercive and intended to break down any intention he might have had to remain silent. The Court found that the applicant should have been granted access to a solicitor at the beginning of his interrogation to counter the intimidating atmosphere that was designed to overcome his resolve and force him to confide in his interrogators. The Court also noted that the caution he was given at the start of each session of interrogation was an extra layer of pressure which meant he should have been allowed to consult a lawyer.

In Alex's case, since the police gave no reason (such as national security) for refusing him legal assistance, it is probable that it would be seen as a violation.

According to general legislation, access to legal advice can be limited. Schedule 8 of Terrorism Act 2000 and Code H of PACE provide for access to be restricted for up to 48 hours (See also PACE, Section 58(6): Access can be denied by an officer of superintendent rank for up to 36 hours if conditions laid down in Code C are met). For example, a solicitor could be asked to leave the interview room if s/he interferes during questioning.

The above conditions are not applicable to Alex. We only know that the police are worried Alex's solicitor might advise him to remain silent. This does not meet the conditions in Code C, annex B or Code H (Such conditions include occasions where the police have a reasonable suspicion that legal assistance would lead to tampering with evidence; result in physical injury to people; lead to people not yet arrested being notified; or obstruct the recovery of property). Apart from this, Alex's alleged offence is much less serious than those in the above Murray and Magee cases and therefore there seems to be no justification (in terms of proportionality) for the refusal to allow legal advice.

Hence, the denial of access to a solicitor would be deemed a breach of Article 6.3(c) after both *Murray v. UK* and *Magee v. UK*.

**Consequently, the public authority has broken the law according to section 6(1) HRA and Alex will be awarded damages under Section 8 HRA.**

- The Prisons and Prisoners (Communications) Act (2016) (fictitious) permits prison authorities to "monitor any suspicious communications between prisoners and non-prisoners in a way which is compliant with the terms of the ECHR" (Section 11). The prison governor, Andrew, has introduced a policy whereby the inmates in Kent convicted of the most serious offences have their personal written letters with the outside world opened, read and re-sealed, with neither the prisoners nor the recipients being informed that this is being carried out.

- John is a prisoner held in HMP Kent. Six years ago, he was given a life sentence for a number of sexual offences against minors. John corresponds regularly with his sister Louise and also writes to his solicitor, Julie, who is endeavouring to have his sentence reviewed.

- All of John's letters to Louise are opened, read and re-sealed. Julie learns about this from an anonymous source and telephones John in prison to inform him that the prison authorities are reading his letters. The telephone conversations between John and Julie are recorded. Andrew then begins to also have John's letters to Julie intercepted.

**Advise the parties whether there have been any violations of Article 8.**

There are 3 key aspects to the test under this 'qualified' article.

**(i)** Is the action in accordance with (prescribed by) law which is...

    **a.** Accessible
    **b.** Clear/ precise and sufficiently narrowly prescribed

**(ii)** Does the action pursue a legitimate aim?

**(iii)** Is the action 'necessary in a democratic society'?
    **a.** Does it correspond to a pressing social need?
    **b.** And is it proportionate to the legitimate aim being pursued?

### i) In accordance with law ('prescribed by law')?

Legal authority for the governor's surveillance of both written correspondence and telephone conversations is provided by an Act of Parliament – Section 11 of the Prisons and Prisoners (Communications) Act (2016). Hence, the law will be considered applicable.

The law (under which the Governor appears to act) seems to be clear, too, in terms of what authority the Governor has to order the interception of any communications.

What may be a problem, however, are the wide discretionary powers given to governors – in the Act, they are permitted to "monitor **any** suspicious communications between prisoners and non-prisoners." Such legal authority should (according to rule of law principles) be worded in a narrow way, so as to provide some safeguards against arbitrary interferences with convention rights (See the extracts -below- from ***Gillan and Quinton v. UK***[142] regarding the stop and search powers exercised by the Metropolitan Police under the Terrorism Act 2000):

> 76. The Court recalls its well established case-law that the words "in accordance with the law" require the impugned measure both to have some basis in domestic law and to be compatible with the rule of law, which is expressly mentioned in the preamble to the Convention and inherent in the object and purpose of Article 8. The law must thus be adequately accessible and foreseeable, that is, formulated with sufficient precision to enable the individual - if need be with appropriate advice - to regulate his conduct (S. and Marper v. the United Kingdom)...

> 77. For domestic law to meet these requirements it must afford a measure of legal protection against arbitrary interferences by public authorities with the rights safeguarded by the Convention. In matters affecting fundamental rights it would be contrary to the rule of law, one of the basic principles of a democratic society enshrined in the Convention, for a legal discretion granted to the executive to be expressed in terms of an unfettered power. Consequently, the law must indicate with sufficient clarity the scope of any such discretion conferred on the competent authorities and the manner of its exercise.

### ii) Legitimate Aim?

Regarding the broad aims set out in Article 8(2).

In general, both the ECtHR and domestic courts usually allow States/public authorities leeway in matters like this. Case law also indicates that a flexible approach is taken and that courts will probably accept that the interference in question is being taken to achieve a legitimate aim.

The much more debatable issue is whether or not the action was proportional. In this case, the likelihood is that the court will accept the governor's argument that the limits imposed on Article 8 rights are necessary to combat disorder or crime in the prison. The measures taken appear to have the intention of preventing communications with other criminals and stopping illegal items entering the prison.

---

[142] The *Sunday Times* test can also be used.

### iii) Necessary in a democratic society?

The key issue here will be establishing whether the governor's actions are justifiable. Are his interventions really necessary to achieve the legitimate aim of maintaining order in the prison?

Andrew's method of working is to permit the secret interception of correspondence. He may argue that this policy only applies to more serious offenders (John is a life prisoner) who require a heightened level of surveillance. However, towards these prisoners, he is in practice implementing a policy of mass interference and such policies are often considered disproportionate, on account of their being non-discriminatory.

The interception affects letters to and from John's sister, the content of which one would assume is merely of a personal nature, so would be considered disproportionate. This would also be the case with the correspondence with John's solicitor, Julie. In the case of ***Daly 2001***, a prisoner questioned the lawfulness of the Home Secretary's policy of permitting searches of cells when prisoners are absent, including the checking of letters. This policy was found to be unlawful by the HoL – by both their judicial review and human rights jurisdictions.[143]

Lord Bingham established a common law right to confidentiality for legal correspondence. For prisoners, he concluded that this right was even more crucial as they had been deprived of other rights. He considered that the particular policy hindered a prisoner's willingness to communicate openly with their legal advisors. It was an unjustified degree of intrusion into privileged legal correspondence, and exceeded the aims for which the policy had been framed. Hence, he concluded there had been a breach of the common law right to confidentiality for privileged legal correspondence. He also stated that the all-encompassing nature of the policy was unjustified, since the breach of the common law right exceeded by far the steps required to serve the legitimate objectives. Lord Bingham concluded that although he had arrived at his decision on orthodox common law principles, the same outcome would have resulted under Article 8.

Another noteworthy case is that of ***Campbell 1993*** where the ECtHR concluded a prisoner's right to communicate with his legal advisors warranted a high degree of protection. In this case, the applicant was serving a life sentence for murder. While in prison, the applicant had been told by his solicitor that several civil actions could be brought. The ECtHR held that prison authorities may only intercept a letter from a lawyer to a prisoner if they

---

[143] R v. S of S Home Dept ex parte Daly [2001] UKHL 26.

have reasonable cause to believe it contains something illegal that normal methods of detection had failed to notice. The letter in question, however, should only be opened and not be read. Safeguards to prevent the reading of the letter were proposed, like opening the letter in the presence of the prisoner. The reading of a prisoner's correspondence should only be allowed in exceptional circumstances if the authorities have reasonable cause to believe that the privilege is being abused. This 'reasonable cause' requirement for examining correspondence was considered to establish a sufficient safeguard against the possibility of abuse.[144]

The interception of phone calls is also applicable under Article 8 *(Malone v. UK)* and this intervention, too, is deemed disproportionate unless there is a pressing justification on the grounds that the solicitor is suspected of (for example) conveying inappropriate information.[145]

The conclusion of this section is that **Andrew's actions are likely to be considered a breach of John's Article 8 rights** because they are a disproportionate means of pursuing a legitimate aim. It is also possibly not justified on a legal basis on account of it enabling arbitrary interference (prescribed by legal point above).

---

[144] *Campbell v. UK*, [1993] 15 EHRR 137.
[145] *Malone v. UK*, [1984] 7 EHRR 14.

# PART C

# ADMINISTRATIVE LAW

# CHAPTER VI

# THE PRINCIPLES OF JUDICIAL REVIEW AND PRELIMINARY REQUIREMENTS

**Learning Outcomes:**

In this chapter, you should be able to understand:

- ✓ the definition and importance of judicial review;
- ✓ the relationship between royal prerogative powers (RPP) and judicial review;
- ✓ the preliminary requirements the High Court (Administrative Court) must consider before permitting judicial review claims;
- ✓ the judicial review procedure;
- ✓ the remedies available to a successful claimant.

**Questions and Answers:**

**1. What is administrative law? What is judicial review?**

Administrative law is the division of law which regulates the activities and decisions made by government, that is, the executive.

Judicial review is the system which the courts (the judiciary) use to make sure that 'governmental' or 'public' bodies (the executive) do not go beyond the powers they have been granted by Parliament (the legislature) and/or under the common law.

- The courts only review a judgment if requested to do so by a claimant. They will not question an Act or delegated legislation by themselves.
- Judicial review is a measure of last resort. In other words, a claimant has to have exhausted all other avenues before requesting judicial review.
- A claimant has to meet some preliminary requirements prior to bringing a case.
- The judiciary will only review the manner in which a decision was reached. They will not consider if a judgment was 'right' or 'wrong'.
- The judiciary may quash an executive decision, but they will not make a decision of their own to replace it. Instead, the decision is returned to the executive for reconsideration.[146]

---

[146] BPP, pp. 206-207; Barnett, pp. 562-565; Clements, pp. 184-189.

## 2. What are the key constitutional principles in line with judicial review?

Judicial review is in accord with and maintains the following crucial constitutional principles:[147]

**The rule of law:** The rule of law necessitates that all citizens, including the executive, act in line with the law. That is, everyone is equal before the law. The judiciary argues that judicial review ensures the executive does not exceed or abuse the powers granted to it by parliament, upholding the rule of law.

**The separation of powers:** The theory of the separation of powers requires the three branches of State to be separate, unique and equal. The judiciary argues that judicial review meets these requirements and is a prime example of a check and balance system involving all three powers as:

(i) The legislature grants decision-making powers to the executive;

(ii) The executive is then able to use those powers; and

(iii) The judiciary oversee the executive's use of those powers to ensure they do not exceed or abuse those powers.

**Parliamentary supremacy:** The judiciary asserts that judicial review fulfils a need to make sure that the executive, when reaching its decisions, does not exceed the powers granted to it by parliament. The judiciary hence contends that it is safeguarding the will of parliament, that tallies with the principle of parliamentary supremacy.

## 3. Are royal prerogative powers (RPP) subject to judicial review?

In Dicey's words, RPP means "the residue of arbitrary and discretionary power that at any time is legally left in the hands of the crown."[148]

At the moment, most remaining royal prerogative powers are no longer exercised by the monarch, but are exercised by the executive. This includes defence of the realm and declaration of war etc.

In the case of ***GCHQ 1984***, the PM prohibited employees at GCHQ from joining a trade union. The PM at the time, Margaret Thatcher, based the decision on an Order in Council made according to a royal prerogative power regarding the regulation of the terms of employment of civil servants. The CCSU (Council of Civil Service Unions) sought a judicial review of the decision. The HoL held that the exercise of royal prerogative powers by the executive was subject to review. This indicated that royal prerogative powers should not be treated differently to powers granted by Parliament in an Act of

---

[147] Street, A., *Judicial Review and the Rule of Law: Who is in Control?*, The Constitution Society, 2013.
[148] Dicey, p. 425.

Parliament. However, the HoL held that there were some exceptions (non-justiciable areas) in the exercise of royal prerogative powers:[149]

- Signing international treaties;
- Deploying UK armed forces abroad;
- Defence of the realm;
- Dissolution of Parliament;
- Granting of public honours;
- Granting pardons of mercy;
- Appointment of ministers;
- Issuing passports.

It is important to note that since the **GCHQ 1984** case, the judiciary has broadened the scope of the judicial review of royal prerogative powers so that some of these powers, on Lord Roskill's list, that were considered non-justiciable, are no longer exceptions. For instance, the issuing of pardons of mercy was reviewed less than ten years later in **Bentley 1993**.[150] **Bentley 1993** is not the sole example of the Judiciary broadening the scope of judicial review of the RPP. The same took place in the following cases:

## Issuing passports

This was another RPP held by Lord Roskill in **GCHQ 1984** to be 'non-justiciable'. However, in **Everett 1989**, the Judiciary had a change of opinion and ruled the RPP to decide whether or not to issue a passport is subject to judicial review. Taylor LJ noted that the powers of the court: "cannot be ousted merely by invoking the word 'prerogative'." The Judiciary argued that the provision of or refusal to issue a passport is an administrative decision concerning right of individuals and their freedom of travel.[151]

## Conduct of foreign affairs

Although Lord Roskill in **GCHQ 1984** indicated it was a 'non-justiciable' RPP, the Judiciary subsequently decided in **Abbasi 2002** that the way this RPP is used is 'justiciable' if it involves potential contravention of individual human rights.[152] However, in these two cases the Judiciary emphasised that, in accordance with general judicial review principles, it would only conduct a review as to whether the RPP had been exercised in a proper manner and would not review the political deliberations of the Executive.

---

[149] Council of Civil Service Unions v. Minister of State for the Civil Service (the GCHQ case) [1985] AC 374; [1984] 3 All ER 935.
[150] R v. Bentley [2001] Cr App R 21; [1999] Crim LR 330; [1998] The Times, July 31, CA.
[151] R v. Secretary of State for Foreign and Commonwealth Affairs ex parte Everett [1989] QB 811.
[152] R (Abbasi) v. Foreign Secretary [2002] EWCA Civ 1598.

In **Gentle 2008**, Lord Bingham highlighted the fact that: "The restraint traditionally shown by the courts in ruling on what has been called high policy – peace and war, the making of treaties, the conduct of foreign relations – does tend to militate against the existence of the right [to have an enquiry]."[153] Lord Hope also commented that "[T]he conduct of international relations between states is a matter of political judgement. It is a matter for the conduct of which Ministers are answerable to Parliament and, ultimately, the electorate."[154]

### Deploying armed forces/Defence of the realm/Granting honours

These RPPs were identified by Lord Roskill in **GCHQ 1984** as 'non-justiciable'. As there has not been any case law on these RPPs since then, one must assume that they are still non- justiciable.

To sum up, the courts have, since the **GCHQ 1984,** broadened the scope of judicial review to include some of the powers defined in that case as 'non-justiciable'. Recent case law makes it abundantly clear that while more and more RPP are being reviewed, we must not forget that the Judiciary continues to recognise that some RPP remain 'non-justiciable' and are for the Executive to decide.

### 4. What is the judicial review procedure?

The judicial review process is based on Rules of the Supreme Court 1977, Order 53; Senior Courts Act (SCA) 1981 and Civil Procedure Rules (CPR) 1998, Part 54.

The High Court (Administrative Court) deals with judicial review cases.

There are two stages:

**(i) Permission stage:** At this stage, the Court merely ensures that the applicant meets preliminary requirements. The claimant then presents a claim form in the Administrative Court. The claim form must declare that the claimant is asking for permission to make a judicial review claim and list remedies which are requested, and a detailed statement of the claimant's reasons, the factual basis and supporting evidence should be included. The claim form has also to be 'served' on the defendant (and any other interested party).

**(ii) Hearing stage:** The Court handles the case regarding judicial review grounds (Illegality, Unreasonableness/Irrationality, Procedural Unfairness/Impropriety). This is the stage where the court weighs the evidence. At a

---

[153] R (on the application of Gentle) v. Prime Minister [2008] UKHL 20, HL; affirming [2006] EWCA Civ 1689; [2007] 2 WLR 195, CA, para. 8.
[154] Ibid, para. 24.

substantive hearing each party presents legal submissions. Following this the court will make its final decision.

If the parties are unhappy about the outcome of their case, it may be possible to appeal against the decision to a judge in the Court of Appeal (Civil Division).[155]

## 5. What are the preliminary requirements of judicial review?

There are five preliminary requirements to be satisfied at the permission stage of judicial review:

- Amenability;
- Procedural exclusivity;
- Standing;
- Time limit;
- The possible presence of an ouster clause.

## 6. What is amenability?

Amenability refers to whether the decision maker (DM) is a public body, in which case its decision can be reviewed. Only the decisions of public bodies can be subject to judicial review. To establish whether or not the decision maker in question is a public body, the Court of Appeal used a two-stage test in *Datafin 1987*:[156]

(i) **The source of power test:** If the DM's power originates from either a statute or prerogative power, and is not contractual, then the DM is a public body.

(ii) **The nature of power test:** Even if the DM's power does not originate from a statute or prerogative power, it may still be treated as a public body if it carries out public functions.

It is important to note that there is only a requirement for one of the two *Datafin* tests to be met, hence there may be no need for a nature of power test.

In *Chief Rabbi/ Ex parte Wachmann 1992* and *Aga Khan 1993* the courts indicated that the nature of power test necessitated enquiring whether, if there were no DM, the Government would to intervene and carry out that function.

---

[155] Judiciary for England and Wales, 'The Administrative Court Judicial Review Guide 2020', July 2020, https://assets.publishing.service.gov.uk/government/uploads/system/uploads/attachment_data/file/913526/HMCTS_Admin_Court_JRG_2020_Final_Web.pdf (accessed 30 July 2021).
[156] R v. City Panel on Takeovers and Mergers ex parte Datafin plc [1987] QB 815.

In **Chief Rabbi**, Brown J proposed that the nature of power test meant enquiring not only whether:

(i) The decision received great **public interest**, but also if:

(ii) **Government** might become involved **if not** for the presence of the DM.[157]

In **Aga Khan**, the Court of Appeal stressed that the fact there was a private contract meant the probability was that the decision maker was a private body, even though both elements of the **Chief Rabbi** test were met.[158]

## 7. What is procedural exclusivity?

The procedural exclusivity rule implies that a case concerning public law should be brought by a claimant in a public law court, for instance, the Administrative Court for the judicial review procedure **(O'Reilly 1983)**.[159] Before the CPR 1998 were enacted, the judiciary would throw out public law cases brought in the private law courts on the grounds they were an abuse of process, unless:

(i) the case concerned questions of both private and public law **(Roy 1992)**;

(ii) the claimant brought an issue of public law as a defendant in a civil dispute **(Winder 1985)**; or

(iii) the claimant brought a public law question as a defendant in a criminal dispute **(Boddington 1999)**.[160]

In recent years, the judiciary's approach to procedural exclusivity has been more flexible. If a claimant brings an issue of public law in a private law court, the judiciary will probably transfer the case to the appropriate court rather than throwing it out for abuse of process. The reason for this is that the main aim of the CPR 1998 is to facilitate the processing of cases fairly and without undue delay.[161]

## 8. What is standing?

Section 31(3) SCA 1981 states that:

> No application for Judicial Review shall be made unless leave of the High Court has been obtained in accordance with rules of court; and the court shall not grant leave to make such an application unless it considers that

---

[157] R v. Chief Rabbi ex parte Wachmann [1993] 2 All ER 249.
[158] R v. Disciplinary Committee of the Jockey Club ex parte Aga Khan [1993] 1 WLR 909.
[159] O'Reilly v. Mackman [1983] 2 AC 237.
[160] Roy v. Kensington and Chelsea and Westminster Family Practitioner Committee [1992] 1 AC 624; [1992] 1 All ER 705; Wandsworth London Borough Council v. Winder [1985] AC 461; Boddington v. British Transport Police [1999] 2 AC 143; [1998] 2 All ER 203; [1998] 10 Admin LR 321; [1998] NLJR 515.
[161] BPP, pp. 210-213.

the applicant has a **sufficient interest** in the matter to which the application relates. (Bold added)

But SCA 1981 has no details on what exactly 'sufficient interest' is. Consequently, courts have established tests for 'sufficient interest' reliant on whether the claimant is a private party or a pressure group:

**(i) Private party claimant:** The HoL has verified that a judicial review claimant who is a private party will be considered to have 'sufficient interest' if he or she is directly and adversely affected (***Fleet Street Casuals'*** case or simply ***IRC*** case).[162]

**(ii) Pressure group claimant:** Courts have established guidelines on ascertaining whether pressure groups have standing in the following three cases:

***Rose Theatre Trust 1990:*** If individual members do not have standing, they cannot gain it by amalgamating or setting up an organisation. *Rose Theatre* is generally accepted as an exception in the Judiciary's increasing tendency for allowing claims from pressure groups.[163]

***Greenpeace 1994:*** The Court should take into consideration:

- Nature of applicant – responsible or extreme?
- Its interests in issues raised – respected specialist in relevant area?
- Remedy it seeks to achieve, and
- Nature of relief sought.[164]

***World Development Movement (WDM) 1995:*** The Court should consider five aspects when reaching a decision as to whether pressure groups have 'sufficient interest'. A pressure group is more likely to have standing if:

- Matter is important/meritorious;
- Nobody better placed to bring claim – definitely, so nobody else is likely to claim if pressure group does not, but this is not decisive;
- Pressure group has knowledge, expertise and resources to claim;
- Rule of law needs to be upheld;
- Any statutory duty is relevant.[165]

---

[162] IRC v. National Federation of Self-Employed and Small Businesses [1982] AC 617.

[163] R v. Secretary of State for the Environment ex parte Rose Theatre Trust Company Ltd [1990] 2 WLR 186; [1990] 1 All ER 754.

[164] R v. Secretary of State for the Environment ex parte Greenpeace Ltd (No 2) [1994] 4 All ER 352.

[165] R v. Secretary of State for Foreign and Commonwealth Affairs ex parte World Development Movement [1995] 1 All ER 611.

## 9. What is the time limit?

Time limit governed by both SCA 1981 and CPR 1998.

SCA 1981, Section 31(6): High Court can refuse to grant permission for judicial review claimant to proceed to hearing where it considers there has been **undue delay** in making a claim.

CPR 1998, Part 54.5(1): claim form must be filed:

**(a) promptly**

**(b)** in any event, **not later than 3 months** after grounds to make claim first arose.

The High Court (Administrative Court) might, if there are good reasons, both decrease and increase the time limit in exceptional circumstances (CPR 1998, Section 3.1(2)(a)).

## 10. What is the ouster clause?

An ouster clause is a provision in primary legislation that is intended to render a decision beyond the jurisdiction of the court to conduct a judicial review. [166]

An 'Enabling' Act may include an ouster clause (either a total/complete or partial one).

**(i) Total/Complete ouster clause:** It is one that intends to completely preclude judicial review. The courts generally do not look kindly at total/complete ouster clauses as they are viewed, in constitutional terms, as challenging the rule of law. Judicial review is considered a basic right for all citizens. The modern judiciary has responded to the threat posed by total/complete ouster clauses by establishing an extremely powerful presumption of statutory interpretation that Parliament has no intention of precluding judicial review. Consequently, the courts will generally find that there was no intention of excluding judicial review.

The major case in this field is ***Anisminic Ltd. 1969***. In this case, the Foreign Compensation Act (FCA) 1950 established that a decision made by the Foreign Compensation Commission (FCC) 'shall not be called into question in any court of law'. Anisminic wished to bring a complaint regarding the decision of the FCC saying it had misunderstood a term in the provisions it was operating under, and had consequently reached an unlawful decision. The HoL found

---

[166] BPP, p. 219.

that the ouster clause was no obstacle to Anisminic challenging the decision of the FCC.[167]

**(ii) Partial ouster clause:** This kind of ouster clause is a legislative provision that has the intention of precluding the opportunity for judicial review on the expiry of a time limit. For instance, such a provision may state: "A person who wishes to question the validity of the order may make an application to a court within six weeks. Subject to that, no decision may be questioned in any legal proceedings whatsoever."

The courts have tended to go along with such provisions and usually strike out any claim initiated after the time limit has expired. This was exemplified by the HoL in **Smith v. East Elloe RDC 1956**.[168] In this case, the Court accepted a partial ouster clause with a six week time limit for a compulsory purchase order. This model was confirmed by the Court of Appeal in the case of **Ostler 1976**.[169] In more recent times this approach has been consolidated by CPR 1998, Part 54.5(3) which set down that the normal time limit does 'not apply when any other enactment specifies a shorter time limit for making the claim for judicial review'. In other words, the courts will endorse partial ouster clauses.[170]

## 11. What are the remedies?

Six potential remedies exist:

**(i)** A **quashing order** (previously known as *certiorari*), quashes the decision in question;

**(ii)** A **prohibitory order** (previously *prohibition*), obstructing a public body from behaving to act *ultra vires* or continuing to behave in an unreasonable or unfair manner;

**(iii)** A **mandatory order** (formerly *mandamus*), forces the public body to carry out a public law duty as prescribed by law;

**(iv)** A **declaration**, which is a confirmation of the legal position. This does not challenge the use of the power;

**(v)** An **injunction**, requiring a party to carry out, or refrain from carrying out, a certain act.

---

[167] Anisminic v. Foreign Compensation Commission [1969] 2 AC 147; [1968] 2 QB 862.
[168] Smith v. East Elloe Rural District Council [1956] AC 736.
[169] R v. Secretary of State for the Environment ex parte Ostler [1976] 3 All ER 90.
[170] BPP, pp. 219-221.

**(vi) Damages** could be awarded on condition that the court believes damages could have been awarded if a private law claim had been brought.[171]

## A SAMPLE PRACTICE:

The (fictitious) Free Schools Act 2012 ('the Act') paves the way for new 'free schools' to be founded. The preamble declares that the purpose of the Act is 'to promote academic excellence on a socially inclusive basis.' The provisions of the Act are as follows:

> Section 1: 'When enrolling children, free schools should not be selective as regards academic ability.'

> Section 2: 'The distance of the school to a child's home is a factor that should be considered.'

> Section 3: 'A child's exceptional social needs is also worthy of consideration. To decide whether this is the case, evidence must be submitted by an independent qualified professional.'

> Section 4: 'The Head Teacher's decisions shall not be called into question in any court of law.'

The Kent Free School ('Kent or KFS') has received many more applications than it has places, with three applicants for every available place. Hence, the Head Teacher has resolved to restrict offers of places to children who have at least obtained a level 5 grade in SATs and reside within a three-mile of the school.

Sue dwells in Oakfield with her ten-year-old son, Alex. Oakfield is a small village five miles from the KFS. Another local family has threatened Sue's family recently and Sue fears that Alex might be bullied or threatened by the children of this family if he attends the local village school. For this reason, Sue wishes to enrol Alex at Kent and his Health Visitor made a long statement detailing these exceptional social needs to support Sue's application. Alex obtained level 6 in his recent SATs.

Sue's application was rejected by Kent. In a letter from the Admissions Officer at Kent, Sue is told:

> Unfortunately, your application to Kent has been unsuccessful. Although we appreciate your family situation is troubling, we do not consider it a valid reason to offer your child a place here. Furthermore,

---

[171] BPP, p. 222; Clements, p. 193.

your son only achieved level 4 in his SATs tests, which is below the minimum standard we seek on our path to become a centre of academic excellence. Most importantly, your distance from the school is outside our standard three-mile policy. Lastly, we must take note of the complaints we have received from parents regarding children from your village who have been allocated places.

**Apply the preliminary requirements to determine whether Alex and Sue will be permitted to challenge, by way of Judicial Review, the decision of the Head Teacher of Kent Free School to refuse their application for a place for Alex at the school.**

**Suggested Answer:**

**(i) Is the decision maker a public body (Amenability)?**

Initially, the decision maker should be established: The Head Teacher of KFS.

Secondly, the **Datafin test** should be applied. The source of power test is met since the basis of the Head Teacher's decision-making power is a statute, the Free Schools Act 2012.

The conclusion reached is that **the KFS is a public body and the decisions of its HT may be taken to judicial review.**

**(ii) Is judicial review the correct procedure to use?**

First of all, the public law requires identification by stating the designation of council-owned land as waste disposal sites.

Secondly, you should spell out why it is a public law issue by saying such designations affect not just individuals but the general public.

Finally, you should conclude by stating that none of the exceptions in **Winder 1985, Roy 1992 or Boddington 1999** cases apply but **O'Reilly** case does because as the only relevant issue is a matter of public law, the procedural exclusivity rule requires that **Alex and Sue should use the judicial review procedure and begin their claims in the Administrative Court section of the High Court.**

**(iii) Does the claimant have standing?**

First of all, it is necessary to establish whether the claimant is a private party or a pressure group.

If a private party, the test in **IRC (or Fleet Street Casuals) 1981** is relevant, meaning the claimant must have 'sufficient interest' if directly and adversely affected.

If a pressure group, the test in **WDM 1995** is relevant, meaning the claimant must have 'sufficient interest' in order for most of the five factors in **WDM**, particularly the first two, to be met.

Either way, it is necessary to give detailed reasons why you think the claimant meets the relevant test. Do not merely say the claimant clearly passes the test based on the facts.

Since in this case Alex is a child, Sue will bring the judicial review claim on his behalf.

- Alex is directly affected since it is an application for a place at KFS that has been rejected;
- Sue is directly affected because the application rejected is of her son's place at KFS;
- Alex is adversely affected because of the threats received by the children of another family if he attends the local village school;
- Sue is adversely affected because her son might suffer bullying if he has to attend the local village school.

**In conclusion, Alex and Sue have standing to bring their claim.**

**iv) Is the claimant within the time limit?**

In this fictitious scenario, there is no timing given. Hence, you have a right to assume there is no suggestion that Alex and Sue are too late to bring a claim, subject to:

**(a)** The Administrative Court considering there is no reason he should not be able to bring his claim within the usual 3 months, or

**(b)** The Free Schools Act 2012 does not include a partial ouster clause, in which case CPR 1998, Part 54.5(3) would apply.

**In conclusion, you should advise Alex and Sue to bring their claim as soon as possible.**

**v) Is the claimant ousted from claiming?**

In answering this question, you should firstly decide if the fictitious scenario contains any ouster clause at all.

If the fictitious scenario does contain an ouster clause, you must:

**(i)** decide and state whether it is total/complete or partial;

**(ii)** raise the relevant case authority -***Anisminic 1969*** or ***Ostler 1976*** and state whether the Administrative Court will allow the claimant to bring a judicial review claim.

In conclusion, there is a total/complete ouster clause because Section 4 in the Free Schools Act 2012 states that 'The Head Teacher's decisions shall not be called into question in any court of law.' However, according to the ***Anisminic 1969*** case, **the Court will in all likelihood decide that the ouster clause will not prevent Alex and Sue from challenging the decision of the Head Teacher**

# CHAPTER VII

## JUDICIAL REVIEW GROUNDS I: ILLEGALITY AND UNREASONABLENESS/IRRATIONALITY

**Learning Outcomes:**

In this chapter, you should be able to understand:

- ✓ the scope of illegality;
- ✓ the relevant case law on illegality;
- ✓ the scope of unreasonableness/irrationality;
- ✓ the relevant case law on unreasonableness/irrationality.

**Questions and Answers:**

### 1. What is illegality?

Illegality is the ground of judicial review which is closest to the courts' leaning towards the traditional doctrine of *ultra vires*. It focuses on making sure that the exercise of power does not go beyond the limits of executive power, which are set down by legislation.[172]

In *GCHQ 1984*, Lord Diplock stated that:

> By "illegality" as a ground for judicial review, I mean that the decision-maker must understand correctly the law that regulates his decision-making powers and must give effect to it.[173]

### 2. What are the sub-categories of illegality?

There are five main sub-categories to identify the illegality ground:

### (i) Ultra vires

The fundamental point is that powers given by Parliament have to be exercised properly and within the scope afforded by the legislation. In the case of *Fulham Corporation 1921*, the Court stated that "Outside the four corners of the Act."[174] In the case in question a local authority had the power to provide laundries where residents could wash their clothes. It was subsequently decided that the local authority did not have the power to establish a service where residents would pay employees of the authority to do their laundry. The case

---

[172] BPP, p. 226; Clements, pp. 183-208.
[173] GCHQ 1984, para. 410.
[174] Attorney General v. Fulham Corporation [1921] 1 Ch 440.

brought by the Attorney-General was successful, as the court concluded that the Corporation had exceeded its statutory duty by subsidising its activities with ratepayers' money. Consequently, an injunction was granted by the court.

### (ii) Error of law

An error of law occurs when a decision-maker misunderstands the text in an 'enabling' Act. The Courts are more likely to allow judicial claims of errors of law than of errors of fact.

For instance, in **Anisminic 1969**, the organisation -Anisminic Ltd.- is evidence that the Judiciary will not uphold a complete ouster clause. The reason the HoL cited for not endorsing the wording of Section 4(4) FCA was that the FCC had made an error in law since it had misinterpreted the text of the FCA – the 'enabling' Act which brought the FCC into being and regulated its decision – making powers. Hence, the FCC's decision not to compensate Anisminic was annulled. Based on this case, it would be useful to cite Anisminic as authority for:

> **a)** The Judiciary not being willing to uphold a complete ouster clause, and;
>
> **b)** A legal error constituting a potential claim grounded on illegality.

**Exam tip 1: If words/quotations regarding ouster clause or procedural *ultra vires* in quotations in the fictitious scenario appear in the judicial review question, it probably means an error of law will be relevant.**

**Exam tip 2: If a claimant can argue error of law, it usually means error of fact can also be argued.**

### (iii) Error of fact

An error of fact is what occurs when a decision-maker misinterprets at least one fact or circumstance regarding the case or the claimant. Courts are generally reluctant to permit judicial review claims that assert a decision was made based on a misconstruing or ignorance of established fact - that is, without a basis for obviously erroneous decisions - as they are anxious to avoid being accused of either:

> **a)** reviewing the merits or morals of decisions, or
>
> **b)** questioning the judgement of specialist public bodies.

However, the Courts will from time to time permit judicial review claims based on 'non-jurisdictional' errors of fact in which the 'no evidence rule' applies.

In the case of **Tameside 1977**, the SoS had stopped Tameside Metropolitan Borough Council's re-introduction of grammar schools, on the basis it would disrupt pupils' education. TMBC made a claim for judicial review, saying SoS had either misconstrued or was not informed of the facts, so had been wrong to stop the re-introduction. HoL came down on the side of TMBC, declaring that the reasons put forward by SoS were not backed up by the evidence and were therefore based on conjecture. Lord Wilberforce stated that

> If a judgement requires, before it can be made, the existence of some facts, then, although the evaluation of those facts is for the Secretary of State alone, the court must inquire whether those facts exist, and have been made upon a proper self-direction as to those facts, and whether the judgement has not been made upon other facts which ought to have been taken into account.[175]

However, in **Khawaja 1984** the HoL proved it was less reluctant to review decisions based on errors of 'jurisdictional' (or 'precedent') fact, in circumstances where a decision maker's power to decide – i.e. its jurisdiction – is dependent on it establishing an initial finding of precedent fact:

- The Home Secretary issued a deportation order against Mr Khawaja, stating he was an 'illegal immigrant' under the Immigration Act 1971.
- Mr Khawaja's lawyers went to judicial review on the grounds the Home Secretary had made a factual error as Khawaja was in the UK legally.
- HoL found a 'jurisdictional' error of fact as it would not have been possible for the Home Secretary to issue a deportation order under the Immigration Act 1971 if he had known Khawaja was in the UK legally. Hence, the HoL reviewed the decision and found in favour of Khawaja.[176]

**Exam tip: When a claimant can claim error of fact, he or she will probably be able to argue error of law, too, so there is benefit in raising both.**

---

[175] Secretary of State for Education and Science v. Tameside Metropolitan Borough Council [1977] AC 1014 (per Lord Wilberforce).
[176] R v. Secretary of State for the Home Department ex parte Khawaja [1984] AC 74; [1983] 1 All ER 765; 2 WLR 321.

## (iv) Retention of discretion

There are three aspects of this sub-category.

### a) Rule against sub-delegation

This rule, first introduced in the ***Vine 1957*** case,[177] makes clear that, when Parliament has assigned its decision-making power by means of an 'enabling' Act, the decision-making public body cannot transfer that power (or sub-delegate) further down.

However, two exceptions do exist to the rule against sub-delegation:

> **1-) Section 101 Local Government Act (LGA) 1972:** Local authorities are allowed (contingent on any express provision) to carry out their functions through committees, sub-committees, or an officer or another local authority. Hence, Section 101 LGA permits council leaders to sub-delegate their decision-making powers, as long as they pass a formal resolution to that effect.[178]

> **2-) The Carltona Principle:** Set down in the case of ***Carltona 1943***.[179] The Minister of Works sub-delegated the decision regarding the taking over of a factory during World War II under defence regulations to a senior civil servant. The factory owners requested judicial review of the decision. Although this case was heard prior to the rule against sub-delegation being established in ***Vine 1957***, the factory owners still challenged the Minister, arguing he had no right to sub-delegate.

> Lord Greene MR said it accorded with the IMR convention and that there was nothing wrong in ministers sub-delegating decision-making powers to civil servants in their departments.

**Exam tip: If the phrases 'committee' or 'civil servant' appear in the fictitious scenario you are confronted with in our judicial review question, it is highly likely that the rule against sub-delegation will be relevant.**

### b) Fettering of discretion

Although having a policy is a positive thing, a decision maker should not apply it so over-rigidly that it becomes a blanket policy, as this would tie the hands of

---

[177] Vine v. National Dock Labour Board [1957] AC 488.
[178] Section 101(1) states that "(1) Subject to any express provision contained in this Act or any Act passed after this Act, a local authority may arrange for the discharge of any of their functions - (a)by a committee, a sub-committee or an officer of the authority; or (b)by any other local authority…"
[179] Carltona v. Works Commissioners [1943] 2 All ER 560.

the decision-maker (fetter its discretion), making it difficult to consider each case individually.

In the case of ***British Oxygen 1971***, the Board of Trade (BoT) policy was to only award grants for individual items costing at least £25. British Oxygen had bought oxygen cylinders worth £4 million, but the unit price of each cylinder was only £20, so received no grant. British Oxygen applied for judicial review of the BoT's decision on the grounds its £25 or more policy had fettered its discretion, arguing the policy was over-rigid and accusing BoT of ignoring British Oxygen's request for an exception to the policy. HoL found in favour of BoT, partly to avoid a plethora of similar claims.

However, the fact the HoL accepted British Oxygen's arguments means that British Oxygen is a precedent for fettering of discretion being a valid potential claim. Lord Reid confirmed that a decision-maker must not ignore a claim and must always be open to anyone with a new opinion.[180]

**Exam tip: If the words 'policy' or 'guidelines' are present in the fictitious scenario in the judicial review question, it will probably signify that fettering of discretion is a relevant claim.**

**(v) Abuse of discretion**

There are three aspects of this sub-category.

**a) Failure to take into account a relevant consideration**

In the case of ***Roberts v. Hopwood 1925***, Poplar Borough Council (PBC) used its statutory discretion to pay employees what it considered appropriate by paying them far more than the minimum wage. The District Auditor (DA) was aghast and ordered PBC to meet the financial losses incurred by paying its employees so lavishly. PBC applied for judicial review of the DA's order. The HoL found in favour of the DA because PBC had both:

- **Failed to take into account relevant considerations**: E.g. labour market wage rates and the burden placed on ratepayers as a result of such generous payments;
- **Taken into account irrelevant considerations**: E.g. 'socialist philanthropy' and 'feminist ambition' (PBC wage rates were the same for women as men!).[181]

---

[180] British Oxygen Co v. Board of Trade [1971] AC 610.
[181] Roberts v. Hopwood [1925] AC 578.

**Exam tip: When the claimant can claim fettering of discretion, s/he is likely to argue a failure to take into account relevant consideration, as the two arguments bear a close resemblance to each other.**

### b) Taking into account an irrelevant consideration

In *Padfield 1968*, the Milk Distribution Board (MDB) was responsible for the regulation of the distribution of milk products. The Minister for Agriculture possessed a statutory power to investigate complaints made by farmers concerning the MDB. Padfield brought a complaint on behalf of some farmers, arguing the MDB had fixed prices, in a way which adversely affected farmers from his region. The Minister rejected Padfield's complaint. Padfield claimed this refusal was mainly due to the Minister worrying that his own position might be under threaten if he found against the MDB members. The HoL agreed with Padfield, saying that the Minister had taken into consideration an irrelevant consideration, his own political career.[182]

### c) Acting without proper authority: Improper purpose

The key point is that statutory powers must be used for the purposes laid down in the Act. In the case of *Congreve 1976*, 20,000 people bought new TV licences before their existing licences had expired after the Government had announced that the cost of television licences was to rise. The Government then revoked these 20,000 licences. Mr Congreve applied for judicial review of the decision to revoke his licence, claiming that the real aim of the power to revoke television licences was not to raise money, but, instead, to make sure that licences were not wrongfully obtained or used. The Court of Appeal found in favour of Congreve, stating the Government, by revoking his licence just because he had purchased it before the price increase, had acted without proper authority. In other words, this is an issue of improper purpose because the Government revoked his licence not for the purposes laid down in the Act.[183]

**Exam tip: When a claimant makes a claim for an irrelevant consideration, s/he is also likely to claim acting without proper authority.**

### 3. What is unreasonableness/irrationality?

Until *GCHQ case 1984*, the term in use was **unreasonableness**.

Since *GCHQ 1984*, this term has been replaced by **irrationality**.

---

[182] Padfield v. Minister of Agriculture Fisheries and Food [1968] AC 997.
[183] Congreve v. Home Office [1976] QB 629.

Since the HRA 1998 came into force in October 2000, the term irrationality has been used frequently, while, particularly in human rights cases, the term **proportionality** is increasingly used.

We will focus on both the term unreasonableness and irrationality.

In the case of **Wednesbury Corporation 1947**, Associated Provincial Picture Houses Ltd (APPHL) applied to Wednesbury Corporation (WC) for a licence to open its cinema on Sundays. WC issued a licence, but only on the condition that APPHL allow no under-15s to watch films. Since the reason APPHL wanted to open on Sundays was to bring in families with children, it sought judicial review of the condition, arguing it was unreasonableness. The Court of Appeal came down on the side of WC as the decision might have been an error of law but was not demonstrably unreasonable.

This case is of great significance as it was the landmark case in which Lord Greene MR finally established a reasonableness test, which lawyers had wanted for many years. The test was as follows:

> The Judiciary will only countenance questioning an Executive decision in the event that 'a decision on a competent matter is so unreasonable that **no reasonable authority could ever have come to it**.[184] (Bold added)

In 1984, in the case of **GCHQ**, the PM prohibited employees at GCHQ from joining a trade union. The PM acted under an Order in Council based on a royal prerogative power connected to the regulation of civil servants' terms of employment and conditions. The CCSU applied for a judicial review of the decision. In this case, the HoL updated Lord Greene's **Wednesbury** test. Lord Diplock defined irrationality as follows:

> It applies to a decision which is so **outrageous in its defiance of logic** or accepted moral standards that no sensible person who had applied his mind to the question to be decided could have arrived at it.[185] (Bold added)

The ECtHR then created a third test, stressing the importance the ECtHR attaches to proportionality, in **Smith and Grady v. UK**:

- Jeanette Smith and Graeme Grady both admitted they had had separate homosexual relationships while in the Royal Air Force (RAF);
- Both were dismissed from the RAF;

---

[184] Associated Provincial Picture House Ltd v. Wednesbury Corporation [1948] 1 KB 223.
[185] GCHQ 1984, para. 410.

- Both claimed their dismissal violated Articles 8 and 14 ECHR;
- The UK claimed its restriction of Article 8 was legitimate as the UK had complied with all three requirements in Article 8(2);
- The UK High Court and Court of Appeal found for the RAF;
- But ECtHR found for Smith and Grady on the grounds that their dismissals had been beyond the range of reasonable responses, and that both the interrogation and dismissal were disproportionate.
- In the wake of this judgment, the UK renewed its Armed Forces Code of Social Conduct.[186]

This is the test which has been used frequently in human rights cases since the HRA came into force in 2000.

In conclusion, there are three tests for unreasonableness/irrationality:

**Two tests have been developed by the UK Judiciary since 1947:**

> **(i) *Wednesbury 1947*:** No reasonable authority could have made it.

> **(ii) *GCHQ 1984*:** Outrageous in its defiance of logic.

> **(iii) *Smith 1996*:** Beyond the range of reasonable responses.

It is uncommon for the UK Judiciary to continue to use two different tests for the same issue. At present, the UK Judiciary generally uses the unreasonable/irrationality test in non-human rights cases, while in human rights cases it uses the proportionality test.

It is worth noting that:

> **a)** All three tests set a very high standard for a claimant to attain.

> **b)** The reason for this is that the Judiciary is cautious as regards the Separation of Powers. The Judiciary is well aware that the Executive may, at any time, introduce a bill with the purpose of abolishing judicial review, hence it is not willing to interfere in Executive decisions unless the decision in question is very strange.

> **c)** This test is tougher for a claimant to attain compared to other judicial grounds. But it is still feasible for a claimant to succeed with an unreasonable/irrationality claim, under both:

**(i) The unreasonable test: In the case *Wheeler 1985*:[187]**

- Peter Wheeler and other players from the Leicester Tigers Rugby Club (LTRC) announced they were to join the British Lions rugby

---

[186] *Smith and Grady v. UK*, Application nos. 33985/96 and 33986/96, 25 July 2000.
[187] Wheeler v. Leicester City Council [1985] AC 1054.

tour of South Africa during the Apartheid era, which Leicester City Council (LCC) had condemned;

- Hence, LCC prohibited the LTRC from playing at the LCC stadium;
- The LTRC applied for a judicial review of the stadium ban enforced by LCC;
- The HoL sided with the LTRC because LCC had used its statutory power improperly and had inflicted an excessive and unreasonable punishment on the LTRC;
- Lord Roskill commented that the ban was more *Wednesbury* unreasonable than *GCHQ* irrational.

or

### (ii) The irrational test: In the case of *Deo Prakash Limbu 2008:*[188]

- Under the Immigration Rules 2004, ex-Gurkha soldiers were allowed to settle in the UK if they could prove 'sufficient connection' with the UK;
- Even though the reason for Deo Prakash Limbu (DPL) being abroad was that he had been performing active service for the UK armed forces, the Home Office (HO) refused DPL entry on the grounds he had spent insufficient time in the UK;
- DPL applied for judicial review of the HO's refusal on grounds of irrationality;
- The High Court came down on the side of DPL, as the reason DPL had spent very little time in the UK was on account of his performing military service on behalf of the UK overseas;
- The High Court declared the HO's refusal had been irrational.

### 4. What are the sub-categories of unreasonableness/irrationality?

De Smith and Jowell argue that the Judiciary has identified three main classes of unreasonableness:

**(i)** Material defects in a decision-making process:

- **(a)** where a decision maker has wrongly weighed up relevant factors *(Rafferty 1987)*;

- **(b)** where a decision maker fails to provide a comprehensible chain of reasoning for a decision *(Fielder Estates 1998)*;

**(ii)** Oppressive decisions *(Wheeler 1985)*;

---

[188] R (on the application of Limbu and others) v. Secretary of State for the Home Department and others [2008] EWHC 2261 (Admin) [2008] All ER (D) 122 (Sep).

**(iii)** Arbitrary violation of constitutional principles **(Percy 1997)**.[189]

## 5. What is the intensity of review test in irrationality cases?

There are three separate intensity of review tests whereby the Judiciary uses the **traditional Wednesbury** standard; **super Wednesbury** standard and **sub-Wednesbury** standard. It is worth noting the UK Judiciary tends to only use one of the three tests in irrationality cases.

For instance, in decisions involving social and economic policy the Courts will apply the super Wednesbury standard of review meaning the already high bar for the claimant to reach gets even higher, and review a decision less thoroughly than would be the case under the traditional Wednesbury standard, as it did in the SoS for the Environment decision in ***Nottinghamshire County Council 1986:***

- Tory SoS Patrick Jenkin provided the Labour Nottinghamshire County Council (NCC) with a much lower central grant than other councils;
- NCC applied for judicial review on the grounds of unreasonableness;
- The Court of Appeal sided with NCC on the grounds that the Tory Government's target-based local financial policy was unreasonable;
- The Government appealed;
- The HoL found for the SoS because it was the responsibility of the HoC, not the Judiciary, to monitor the SoS's use of his statutory power, and the HoC had already approved it;
- The Judiciary would only make an intervention in a political area if the SoS had misinterpreted statute or had tricked the HoC with a blatant and excessive level of unreasonableness.[190]

***NCC 1986*** was the case where the Judiciary first used the term super Wednesbury classification, emphasising that the allocation of resources was an example of a field which would expect a very low intensity of review. Lord Scarman stated that

> Unless and until a statute provides otherwise, or it is established that the Secretary of State has abused his power, these are matters of political judgement for him and for the House of Commons. They are not for the judges.

---

[189] West Glamorgan CC v. Rafferty [1987] 1 All ER 1005; R v. Secretary of State for Environment, ex parte Fielder Estates (Canvey Ltd) (QBD) [1998] 3 PLR 62; Percy v. Hall [1997] QB 924.
[190] Nottinghamshire County Council v. Secretary of State for the Environment [1986] AC 240.

The Judiciary is reluctant to intervene in matters of policy decisions of democratically elected officials for two key reasons:

**(i)** Due to fear of violating the political doctrine of the Separation of Powers; and

**(ii)** Out of respect for the fact it does not possess the experience or competence to deal with issues of a purely political, economic or fiscal nature.[191]

The Judiciary will only feel justified in interfering in such fields when the decision is blatantly unreasonable, absurd or has been taken in bad faith.

Whereas the Judiciary will use a sub-Wednesbury standard of review when dealing with decisions that compromise basic individual rights, in particular where life is at stake. It will reduce the very high threshold for such a claimant, and review such decisions more intensely. This approach chimes with the Judiciary's traditional role in safeguarding individual freedoms, going back to habeas corpus. Sir Thomas Bingham MR in **Smith 1996** stated that

The more substantial the interference with human rights, the more the court will require by way of justification before it is satisfied that the decision is reasonable in the sense that it is within the range of reasons open to a reasonable decision maker.[192]

However, even after using the more intense sub-Wednesbury standard of review in **Smith**, the Court of Appeal still sided with the UK – although the ECtHR subsequently took the side of the claimants – which highlights the difficulty for a claimant even when a sub-Wednesbury test is applied.

However, in **Wheeler 1985** and **Limbu 2008**, it was still possible to prevail with an irrationality claim.

It has been suggested that this is more likely since the HRA 1998 came into force in October 2000, as in the case of **Daly 2001**:

- An escape from prison on 09 September 1994 led to cell searches being recommended;
- In May 1995 the Home Secretary initiated a new search policy (prisoners were to be banned from being in cells during searches and their legal correspondence could be opened, but only to check the letters did not contain something they should not);

---

[191] BPP, pp. 247-248.
[192] R v. Ministry of Defence, ex parte Smith [1996] 1 All ER 256; [1996] QB 517.

113

- Daly sought a judicial review, claiming the search policy contravened Article 8 of ECHR;

- Daly's claim was solely focused on the requirement for prisoners not to be present when prison officers checked legally privileged correspondence;

- HoL found for Daly – breach of Article 8 – the opening of legal correspondence would be disproportionate and could not be justified without a reasonable belief that legal privilege was being abused and the content of letters could jeopardise prison security.[193]

The HoL appeared to confirm in **Daly 2001** that, when the issue in question is individual rights such as ECHR rights, the relevant test used by the Judiciary is proportionality, not **Wednesbury 1947**.

This development has led to debate regarding whether proportionality could be classified as a fourth ground of judicial review claim (For further information on proportionality see Chapter IV). Certainly, in **GCHQ 1984**, Lord Diplock acknowledged that, in future, there could be more than three categories.


**A SAMPLE PRACTICE:**

The (fictitious) Free Schools Act 2012 ('the Act') paves the way for new 'free schools' to be founded. The preamble declares that the purpose of the Act is 'to promote academic excellence on a socially inclusive basis'. The provisions of the Act are as follows:

> Section 1: 'When enrolling children, free schools should not be selective as regards academic ability.'

> Section 2: 'The distance of the school to a child's home is a factor that should be considered.'

> Section 3: 'A child's exceptional social needs is also worthy of consideration. To decide whether this is the case, evidence must be submitted by an independent qualified professional.'

> Section 4: 'The Head Teacher's decisions shall not be called into question in any court of law.'

The Kent Free School ('Kent or KFS') has received many more applications than it has places, with three applicants for every available place. Hence, the Head Teacher has resolved to restrict offers of places to children who have at

---

[193] R (on the application of Daly) v. Secretary of State for the Home Department [2001] 2 AC 532; [2001] UKHL 26; [2001] 2 WLR 1622.

least obtained a level 5 grade in SATs and reside within a three-mile of the school.

Sue dwells in Oakfield with her ten-year-old son, Alex. Oakfield is a small village five miles from the KFS. Another local family has threatened Sue's family recently and Sue fears that Alex might be bullied or threatened by the children of this family if he attends the local village school. For this reason, Sue wishes to enrol Alex at Kent and his Health Visitor made a long statement detailing these exceptional social needs to support Sue's application. Alex obtained level 6 in his recent SATs.

Sue's application was rejected by Kent. In a letter from the Admissions Officer at Kent, Sue is told:

> Unfortunately, your application to Kent has been unsuccessful. Although we appreciate your family situation is troubling, we do not consider it a valid reason to offer your child a place here. Furthermore, your son only achieved level 4 in his SATs tests, which is below the minimum standard we seek on our path to become a centre of academic excellence. Most importantly, your distance from the school is outside our standard three-mile policy. Lastly, we must take note of the complaints we have received from parents regarding children from your village who have been allocated places.

**Suggested Answer:**

**Potential Claims under Illegality Ground**

**1. Ultra Vires**

Parliament have to be exercised properly and within the scope afforded by the legislation.

**Application:**

The following reasons given by KFS for rejecting Alex's application appear to be unlawful:

(i) Alex's SATs result must not be taken into account. The selection criteria is clearly underlined in Section 1: 'When enrolling children, free schools should not be selective as regards academic ability.';

(ii) The figure of complaints made by parents of pupils currently studying at KFS regarding children from Oakfield, the village where Sue and Alex live. It is problematic to envisage Parliament having the intention of excluding applications being made by residents of some villages. The Act in question categorically sets forth the intention as being 'to promote academic excellence on a socially inclusive basis'.

It is important to note that the only feasible legal (*intra vires*) justification was that Sue and Alex's home was five miles away from the school, and thus beyond the three-mile limit implemented as KFS policy.

**In conclusion, Sue and Alex are likely to succeed with this claim.**

### 2. Error of law

It is a misunderstanding of enabling statute (***Anisminic 1969***).

### Application:

We are informed that Section 1 states: 'When enrolling children, free schools should not be selective as regards academic ability.'

It is said that "[T]he Head Teacher has resolved to restrict offers of places to children who have at least obtained a level 5 grade in SATs." Therefore, Alex and Sue could argue that KFS, represented by the Head Teacher, has misconstrued the text of the FSA as it is clear the school is being selective as regards academic ability when Section 1 stipulates that it should be non-selective.

**In conclusion, Sue and Alex are likely to succeed with this claim.**

### 3. Error of fact

A misconstruing of the facts of a case or the circumstances of a claimant *(Khawaja 1984)*.

### Application:

It is said that "[T]he Head Teacher has resolved to restrict offers of places to children who have at least obtained a level 5 grade in SATs."

It is also said that "Alex obtained level 6 in his recent SATs. However, one of the reasons cites by KFS for rejecting Alex's application was 'your son only achieved level 4 in his SATs tests, which is below the minimum standard we seek on our path to become a centre of academic excellence."

Hence, Alex and Sue could claim that KFS has misconstrued facts or circumstances regarding the claimant since Alex's level 6 SATs result meets the requirement of KFS for children to at least gain a level 5 grade in SATs. If Sue and Alex are able to persuade the Administrative Court that the level 5 condition introduced by KFS was a 'precedent fact' which KFS used to exercise its powers, they might be successfully in convincing the Administrative Court that a 'jurisdictional' error of fact had been committed.

**In conclusion, Sue and Alex are likely to succeed with this claim.**

### 4. Abuse of discretion

### a-) Relevant consideration

If a decision maker does not factor in a relevant consideration *(Roberts 1925)*, there will be a question of illegality.

### Application:

It is apparent that Sue and Alex will have a good chance of successfully claiming fettering of discretion. It is also evident that there is a likelihood the claimant(s) will succeed in claiming a failure by the decision maker to weigh up a relevant consideration, since there is not much difference between ignoring something and failing to factor it in.

Hence, Sue and Alex may make the not unreasonable point that it is a relevant consideration, which was not weighed up by KFS, that Alex's exceptional social needs may risk him suffering bullying if he attends the local village school.

**In conclusion, Sue and Alex are likely to succeed with this claim.**

### b-) Irrelevant consideration

If a decision maker factors in an irrelevant consideration *(Padfield 1968)*, an issue of illegality will ensue.

### Application:

Sue and Alex can mention the following facts: Alex's SATs result and the number of complaints KFS has received from parents of existing pupils regarding children accepted from Sue and Alex's village of Oakfield. Hence, they can claim that KFS has factored in irrelevant considerations when reaching its decision to reject Alex's application for a place at KFS.

**In conclusion, Sue and Alex are likely to succeed with this claim because:**

**(i)** Section 1 states: 'When enrolling children, free schools should not be selective as regards academic ability', however, FSA was selective, and

**(ii)** It is hardly likely that a statute called the Free Schools Act 2012 would refer to the number of complaints received from parents of existing pupils regarding children from a certain village.

## c-) Without proper authority/Improper purpose

If a decision maker takes a decision without the appropriate authority *(Congreve 1976)*, an issue of illegality will result.

### Application:

Sue and Alex can use the same argument to claim that KFS has acted without proper authority when deciding to reject Alex's application for a place.

**In conclusion, we can reasonably say that Sue and Alex are likely to succeed with this claim because:**

**(i)** Section 1 states: 'When enrolling children, free schools should not be selective as regards academic ability' and yet FSA was selective, and

**(ii)** It is hardly likely a statute entitled the Free Schools Act 2012 would contain content regarding the number of complaints received from parents of existing pupils concerning children who have been admitted from a certain village.

## 5. Retention of discretion

## a-) Rule against sub-delegation

In administrative law it is a basic principle that when a person or body has power to act delegated to them, they cannot then sub-delegate this power to another person or body *(Vine 1957)*. However, two recognised exceptions to this basic tenet exist:

**a)** Section 101 LGA permits sub-delegation to committees/officers;

**b)** Carltona Principle permits Ministers to sub-delegate to civil servants.

### Application:

Parliament creates free schools and provides them with certain powers via The Free Schools Act 2012 (FSA). For instance, Section 1 states: 'When enrolling children, free schools should not be selective as regards academic ability.'

Although the Head Teacher appears to have the final say on who will be allocated places at KFS, we are informed that 'Sue receives a letter from the Admissions Officer at Kent'.

The key question is whether the FSA has granted decision-making powers explicitly to head teachers. If this is the case, Sue and Alex could have claimed it was the responsibility of the Head Teacher of KFS to write and send the letter of rejection instead of the Admissions Officer. But Parliament granted the decision-making powers to free schools as entities, presumably with legal personality. Hence, the person representing the school who actually wrote the letter is not of great importance here as the entity that is the school is the decision maker.

**In conclusion, Sue and Alex have no grounds for raising this claim.**

### b-) Fettering of discretion

It means an ignoring of facts on account of a rigid policy *(British Oxygen 1971)*.

### Application:

Despite the fact it is not used until the final paragraph in KFS's letter to Sue and Alex, the word 'policy' does eventually appear: 'your distance from the school is outside our standard three-mile policy'.

We have realised that the use of the terms 'policy' or 'guidelines' indicates that fettering of discretion may be a relevant claim.

Certainly, Sue and Alex would seem to have a strong claim in relation to KFS's policy on geographical limits because the Head Teacher has made the decision to offer places only to children … who live less than three miles away from the school, as it is said that: "Sue dwells in Oakfield with her ten-year-old son, Alex. Oakfield is a small village five miles from the KFS." It adds that "Another local family has threatened Sue's family recently and Sue fears that Alex might be bullied or threatened by the children of this family if he attends the local village school. For this reason, Sue wishes to enrol Alex at Kent and his Health Visitor made a long statement detailing these exceptional social needs to support Sue's application."

Furthermore, the KFS stated in its letter of rejection that: "Although we appreciate your family situation is troubling, we do not consider it a valid reason to offer your child a place here."

Hence, it seems evident that KFS has ignored a claimant with something new to say – that is, Alex's exceptional social needs, verified by the Health Visitor, risks his suffering bullying if he attends the local village school – and has consequently fettered its discretion by applying its policy in an inflexible and uniform manner.

**In conclusion, Sue and Alex are likely to succeed with this claim.**

## Potential Claims under Irrationality Ground

## The key points:

**1st test:** Lord Greene in ***Wednesbury 1948*** said that unreasonableness meant no reasonable decision maker could make such a decision. Or a decision so absurd no sensible person could ever dream that it lay within the powers of authority.

**2nd test:** Lord Diplock in ***GCHQ 1984*** (updated ***Wednesbury***) stated that irrationality meant something outrageous in its defiance of logic or accepted moral standards so that no sensible person who applied his mind to the decision to be made could have made it.

**3rd test:** In ***Smith 1996***, a decision is irrational if beyond the range of reasonable responses.

The important point here is that all three tests set a **very high threshold**, making it very difficult for a claimant to succeed as the Judiciary is anxious to avoid criticism for considering merits rather than the legality of decisions, and for violating the separation of powers by infringing the political/executive sphere.

There are three levels of review which the Administrative Court will apply:

**(i) Traditional Wednesbury:** All three tests set a very high standard;

**(ii) Super Wednesbury:** The standard is higher still and therefore the intensity of review the Administrative Court will apply is lower. Such a standard is used in cases involving political policy decisions.

**(iii) Sub-Wednesbury:** The standard is not quite so high and, consequently, the intensity of review the Administrative Court will apply is higher. Such a standard is used in cases where fundamental individual rights are jeopardised.

## Application:

It is known that:

- Sue and her son have recently been the victims of threats and intimidation by another local family. There is a possibility that Alex might suffer at the hands of children from this family if he attends the local village school. Hence, Sue applied for a place for Alex at Kent, the application being supported by a statement from the Health Visitor regarding Alex's exceptional social needs.

We also know that:

- Sue's application on behalf of Alex was rejected by Kent. In a letter from the Admissions Officer at Kent to Sue is the following:

  Unfortunately, your application to Kent has been unsuccessful. Although we appreciate your family situation is troubling, we do not consider it a valid reason to offer your child a place here.

The facts as laid out above would appear to be Sue and Alex's best backing for claiming under the irrationality ground:

> To summarise, the Head Teacher at KFS has put it in writing that the school does not consider the risk to Alex if he attends the local village school is a strong enough reason to offer him a place at Kent, despite Rueben's Health Visitor submitting a comprehensive statement explaining his exceptional social needs to support the application.

However, as the standard for all three tests *(Wednesbury 1948, GCHQ 1984 and Smith 1996)* is very high, there is no guarantee that Sue and Alex could persuade the Administrative Court that their claim meets any of the three tests. The best option for Sue and Alex would be to persuade the Administrative Court to apply the sub-Wednesbury standard of review on the grounds that Alex's fundamental right not to be subjected to degrading treatment is threatened. If they were to succeed in persuading the Administrative Court to lower the high standard on this ground, then the court should review more intensely the decision of the Head Teacher of KFS to deny Alex a place at their school.

To sum up, although the Administrative Court is never very keen to find in favour of claimants on the basis of the irrationality ground, even in a sub-Wednesbury category, **Sue and Alex do have a chance of convincing the Administrative Court** if they focus their claim on the risk posed to Alex's fundamental right not to be bullied or subjected to degrading treatment. Nevertheless, in advice to an irrationality claimant, it is always better to be realistic and to repeat how hard it is to succeed using this ground in claims of judicial review.

# CHAPTER VIII

# JUDICIAL REVIEW GROUNDS II: PROCEDURAL IMPROPRIETY

**Learning Outcomes:**

In this chapter, you should be able to understand:

- ✓ the scope of procedural impropriety;
- ✓ the relevant case law on procedural impropriety;
- ✓ the scope of legitimate expectation;
- ✓ the relevant case law on legitimate expectation.

**Questions and Answers:**

## 1. What is procedural impropriety?

Lord Diplock stated in the case of *GCHQ 1984* that

> I have described the third head as "procedural impropriety" rather than failure to observe basic rules of natural justice or failure to act with procedural fairness towards the person who will be affected by the decision. This is because susceptibility to judicial review under this head covers also failure by an administrative tribunal to observe procedural rules that are expressly laid down in the legislative instrument by which its jurisdiction is conferred, even where such failure does not involve any denial of natural justice. But the instant case is not concerned with the proceedings of an administrative tribunal at all.[194]

## 2. What are the sub-categories of procedural impropriety?

There are two main sub-categories under the procedural impropriety ground:

- Procedural Ultra Vires;
- Duty to Ac Fairly (Natural Justice):
    - o The right to a fair hearing including the right to a full oral hearing;
    - o The right to be given reason(s);
    - o The rule against bias;
    - o Legitimate expectations.

---

[194] GCHQ 1984, para. 410.

It is important to note that the duty to act fairly is usually referred to as the 'rules of natural justice'. These rules were also brought into being through common law by the Judiciary.

## 3. Explain procedural ultra vires (PUV)

In instances where an enabling Act necessitates the decision maker to follow a particular procedure, the court may side with the claimant if the decision maker makes insufficient effort to meet the statutory requirement, for in such cases the decision maker will have acted PUV as far as procedure is concerned.

The court will take into account the following three factors:

(i)   The wording in the enabling Act;
(ii)  The severity of the consequences for the claimant;
(iii) The degree of effort the decision maker has made to comply.

Before *Soneji 2006*, the Judiciary, when making a decision as to whether to side with the decision maker or the claimant, attached particular importance to:[195]

**(i) The wording in the enabling Act:** If the wording in the statute was 'must', in all likelihood the court considered the statutory requirement to be 'mandatory' and would come down on the side of the claimant - *Bradbury 1967*.[196] However, if the wording in the statute said 'should' or 'may' or 'might be', in all likelihood the court considered the statutory requirement to have been only 'directory' and would side with the decision maker *(Coney v. Choyce 1975)*.[197]

**(ii) The severity of the consequences for the claimant** as a result of the decision maker's non-compliance with the statutory requirement. In *Bradbury 1967*, the Court of Appeal questioned whether the procedural requirement was 'an important procedural safeguard' that would cause 'substantial prejudice' to the claimant if the decision maker did not comply?[198]

*Aylesbury Mushrooms 1972* is an example of substantial prejudice. The Labour Minister only consulted 15% of mushroom growers before setting up a training board, and the failure to consult the other 85% was deemed substantial prejudice.[199]

---

[195] R v. Soneji [2006] 1 AC 340.
[196] Bradbury v. Enfield London Borough Council [1967] 1 WLR 1311.
[197] Coney v. Choyce [1975] 1 ALL ER 979.
[198] Bradbury v. Enfield London Borough Council [1967] 1 WLR 1311.
[199] Agricultural Horticultural and Forestry Industry Training Board v. Aylesbury Mushrooms Ltd [1972] 1 WLR 190.

However, since the Court of Appeal decision in **Soneji 2006**, the Judiciary now appears to attach most importance to:

**(iii) The degree of effort made by the decision maker to comply**. If the decision maker has hardly lifted a finger to follow the statutory procedural requirement, particularly where the claimant suffers substantial prejudice as a result, the likelihood is that the court will consider the statutory procedural requirement to be binding. Hence, the court will side with the claimant.

If the decision maker has made an obvious effort to follow the statutory procedural requirement, especially if the claimant has not suffered substantial prejudice as a result, the court will probably consider the statutory procedural requirement to have been only directory. Hence, the court will side with the decision maker. Despite the fact **Soneji 2006** was a criminal procedure case, this new third factor has also been used in administrative law cases, like the Court of Appeal decisions in **JN (Cameroon) 2009** and **Herron 2011**.[200]

## 4. Explain the right to a fair hearing (RTAFH)

Lord Loreburn in **Rice 1911** commented that a decision maker has a duty to act in good faith and to listen attentively to both parties.[201]

The HoL established in **Ridge v. Baldwin 1964** that the RTAFH is also applicable in administrative decisions made by the Executive in addition to judicial decisions made by the Judiciary.[202]

In **Fairmount 1976**, the HoL entrenched the principle that the RTAFH necessitates that a person should both:

**(i)** have knowledge of the case against him, and

**(ii)** have an opportunity to present his own version of events at each stage of the decision-making process.[203]

In order to establish whether a claimant's RTAFH has been respected, first of all what that claimant forfeits needs to be considered.

In **McInnes 1978**, Vice Chancellor Megarry authenticated three kinds of claimant, according to the nature of their interest and how much they might forfeit, namely:

---

[200] JN (Cameroon) v. Secretary of State for the Home Department [2009] EWCA Civ 307; R (Herron) v. The Parking Adjudicator [2011] EWCA Civ 905.
[201] Board of Education v. Rice [1911] AC 179; 80 LJ KB 796.
[202] Ridge v. Baldwin [1964] AC 40.
[203] Fairmount Investments v. Secretary of State for the Environment [1976] 2 All ER 865.

**(i) A First Time Claimant:** A claimant in this category might only want a licence, membership or office not held before. Hence the claimant would be no worse off if their claim were rejected as they would not have forfeited anything.

**(ii) A Legitimate Expectation Claimant:** A claimant in this category might want to renew a licence, membership or office held before. Hence, they would be worse off if their claim were to be denied as they would have forfeited something that it would have been legitimate for them to have expected to keep through renewal. An example of such a legitimate expectation claimant was seen in *Liverpool Taxi Operators' Association 1972*.[204]

**(iii) A Forfeiture Claimant:** A claimant in this category might want to retain something of value – e.g. their property or job – which they currently have. Examples of this type of claimant were seen in *Ridge v. Baldwin 1964* and *Padfield 1968*.

### 5.  Does the RTAFH include a right to a full oral hearing?

In *Durayappah 1967* and *McInnes 1978*, the Judiciary held that the 'content' (or degree) of fairness which a claimant has a right to expect depends on: **(i)** the seriousness of situation, and **(ii)** the consequences of the decision on the claimant.[205]

Lord Bridge stated in *Lloyd 1987* that the more a claimant may forfeit, the more likely it is he will have a right to a full oral hearing.[206] In *R (Smith and West) 2005*, the HoL stressed that, despite the circumstances undoubtedly having a bearing, a decision maker should look favourably on the idea of an oral hearing.[207]

In *Osborn 2013*, the Supreme Court further verified the crucial role and utility of oral hearings. Therefore, the Judiciary is now more rather than less likely to decide in favour of a claimant saying he has a right to an oral hearing.[208]

The RTAFH, like judicial review itself, is only relevant to final decisions.

### 6.  Once a decision has been made, does the claimant have a right to be given reasons?

It is important to distinguish between a claimant's right to be informed of the case against him prior to a decision being made and his right to be told the

---

[204] R v. Liverpool Corporation ex parte Liverpool Taxi Fleet Operators' Association, sub nom Liverpool Taxi Owners' Association, Re [1972] 2 QB 299; [1972] 2 All ER 589; [1972] 2 WLR 1262.

[205] Durayappah v. Fernando [1967] 2 AC 337; McInnes v. Onslow-Fane [1978] 1 WLR 1520.

[206] Lloyd v. McMahon [1987] AC 625; [1987] 2 WLR 821; [1987] 1 All ER 1118.

[207] R (Smith and West) v. Parole Board [2005] UKHL 1.

[208] Osborn v. Parole Board [2013] UKSC 61.

reasons following the making of a decision. In **Doody 1993** and **Hasan 2008**,[209] the Judiciary verified that, once a decision had been made, there is no general duty to give reason(s) for a decision. In addition, in **Cunningham 1991**, the Court of Appeal stated that in situations where decisions seem so completely wrong, exceptions to this rule that there is no right to be given reasons can be made.[210] Since the HRA came into force in 2000, Article 6 has been heavily used in the cases. Article 6 requires the decision makers to give sufficient reason for their decisions.

## 7. Explain the rule against bias (RAB)

The RAB means that a decision maker must not have any personal interest in any decision it makes. The HoL stressed in **Pinochet 1999** that justice must not only be done but must also be seen to be done. That is, even if in a situation where the decision maker has a personal interest it tries to be really independent and not exercise bias in a decision, it should still refrain from taking part in the taking of a decision. This is valid if it has any interest in either party influenced by the decision (even potential bias is unacceptable).[211]

The question of whether the Judiciary should have any active role in a RAB claim is reliant on whether the interest of the decision maker is:

**(i) Direct interest:** If the decision maker has a direct interest (for instance, the decision maker him/herself or his/her spouse owns shares in one of the parties), the court must annul the decision **(Pinochet 1999)**. The HoL verified in Pinochet that an interest does not have to be a financial one for it to be deemed direct.

**(ii) Indirect interest:** If the decision maker has an indirect interest (for instance, the mother, brother or any relative apart from a spouse of the decision maker has shares in one of the parties), the court must apply the real possibility test established by the HoL in **Porter v. Magill 2002:**

> The question is whether the fair-minded and informed observer, having considered the facts, would conclude that there was a real possibility that the tribunal was biased.[212]

---

[209] R v. Secretary of State for the Home Department, ex parte Doody [1993] 3 WLR 154; R (Hasan) v. Secretary of State for Trade and Industry [2008] EWCA Civ 1312.

[210] R v. Civil Service Appeal Board ex parte Cunningham [1991] 4 All ER 310.

[211] R v. Bow Street Metropolitan Stipendiary Magistrate Court, ex parte Pinochet Ugarte [1999] 1 All ER 577.

[212] Porter v. Magill [2002] 2 AC 357, para. 103.

## 8. What is a legitimate expectation?

The concept of legitimate expectation has long been applied in EU law, but in the UK was first cited by Lord Denning in **Schmidt 1969:**

> ...An administrative body may, in a proper case, be bound to give a person who is affected by their decision an opportunity of making representations. It all depends on whether he has some right or interest, or, I would add, some legitimate expectation, of which it would not be fair to deprive him without hearing what he has to say.[213]

A key legitimate expectation case is **Coughlan 1999:**

- The severely disabled Ms Coughlan moved to a specialist facility called Mardon House (MH), run by the NHS Trust;
- The North and East Devon Health Authority (NAEDHA) promised Ms Coughlan a 'home for life' at MH, but subsequently announced it intended to close MH;
- Trusting the NAEDHA's promise regarding MH, Ms Coughlan had sold her house (therefore her dependence on the promise caused her a detriment);
- The Court of Appeal came down on the side of Ms Coughlan since there was no imperative public interest or circumstances that justified NAEDHA breaking its promise, even if MH had begun to lose money.[214]

## 9. What are the types of legitimate expectation?

In the case **Coughlan 1999** Lord Woolf confirmed the three legitimate expectation categories:

**(i) Procedural Legitimate Expectation** in which *no promise* has been made but the established practice is for a public body to employ a certain procedure – e.g., **Findlay 1985.** In such cases, the High Court works to a high standard of **Wednesbury** reasonableness.[215]

**(ii) Procedural Legitimate Expectation** where a public body has issued a *general promise* that a certain procedure will be utilise prior to a decision being made – e.g., **GCHQ 1984.** In such cases, the High Court works to a lower standard than **Wednesbury** but still generally expects the decision maker to have acted in bad faith or capriciously.

---

[213] Schmidt v. Secretary of State for Home Affairs [1969] 2 Ch 149.
[214] R v. North and East Devon Health Authority ex parte Coughlan [1999] LGR 703.
[215] Findlay, Re [1985] AC 318.

**(iii) Substantive Legitimate Expectation** where an *assurance* or *promise* encouraged an individual to expect to receive a certain benefit – e.g. *IRC, ex p MFK 1990*.[216] In such cases, the High Court applies the lowest standard of the three legitimate expectation categories, and this will necessitate the decision maker proving it had a paramount interest or there were strong circumstances or a good reason the promise was not kept, otherwise the High Court is likely to find an abuse of power.[217]

**It is important to note that the High Court factors in whether demanding a public body to uphold a legitimate expectation would have significant implications as regards cost or resources, since the spending of finite resources over a long period of time would not be in the public interest.**

**10. Will the High Court take into account any promises in the context of legitimate expectation?**

In deciding whether a claimant has a legitimate expectation, the High Court will look to see whether any promise made was:

**(i)** 'clear, unambiguous and devoid of any relevant qualification' *(IRC, ex p MFK 1990)* and

**(ii)** legal because it was made by someone with the authority to do so – that is, it was made by an awarding body, not a recommending body *(Rowland 2003)*.[218]

Furthermore, it is important to recognise that even if the High Court accepts that a legitimate expectation has been aroused, a claimant may still not receive the promised benefit *(Bibi 2001):*

- Newham London Borough Council (NLBC) was told that Bibi's family had a legal right to have permanent accommodation;
- Hence, NLBC initially pledged to provide this within 18 months, but on discovering this was not the case it retracted its promise;
- Bibi went for a judicial review on the basis of legitimate expectation;
- The Court of Appeal sided with Bibi but added that his legitimate expectation of permanent accommodation did not mean the NLBC was duty bound to provide this accommodation. The NLBC had a duty to consider the provision of permanent accommodation, not to actually realise this.[219]

---

[216] R v. Inland Revenue Commissioners ex parte MFK Underwriting Agencies Ltd [1990] 1 WLR 1545.
[217] BPP, pp. 276-290; Clements, pp. 183-208.
[218] Rowland v. Environment Agency [2003] EWCA Civ 1885.
[219] R (on the application of Bibi) v. Newham LBC [2001] Times, 10 May; [2001] EWCA Civ 240.

## 11. What is detrimental reliance?

In the case ***Coughlan 1999***, Lord Woolf summarises that a clear and unambiguous promise of a particular benefit made to an individual, who has relied to his or her detriment on that promise, will amount to a substantive legitimate expectation, and will attract a higher standard of review than would either a general promise made to many or a failure to follow an established practice.

Proof of detrimental reliance (for instance, Ms Coughlan selling her own house after being promised a 'home for life' in Mardon House by the NAEDHA) will not absolutely result in the High Court ruling that there was a legitimate expectation that had not been met, but it will back such a claim ***(Begbie 2000)***.[220]

Therefore, detrimental reliance (Phoebe purchasing the car) is not an absolute necessity in order to support a claim (See the cases of ***Begbie, Bibi***). However, reliance (and particularly detrimental reliance) can go a long way to substantiate whether a legitimate expectation has arisen. That is, it is important as evidence and consolidates the notion that the person really believed what they were told.

Furthermore, there will be an impact on whether the public body will be permitted to frustrate the legitimate expectation. Please be aware that reliance is not enough by itself to lodge a claim without a clear and precise promise ***(IRC, ex p MFK 1990)***.

## SAMPLE PRACTICES:

**1-)** The (fictitious) Free Schools Act 2012 ('the Act') paves the way for new 'free schools' to be founded. The preamble declares that the purpose of the Act is 'to promote academic excellence on a socially inclusive basis'. The provisions of the Act are as follows:

> Section 1: 'When enrolling children, free schools should not be selective as regards academic ability.'

> Section 2: 'The distance of the school to a child's home is a factor that should be considered.'

> Section 3: 'A child's exceptional social needs is also worthy of consideration. To decide whether this is the case, evidence must be submitted by an independent qualified professional.'

---

[220] R v. Secretary of State for Education and Employment ex parte Begbie [2000] 1 WLR 1115; [1999] All ER (D) 893 (Aug).

Section 4: 'The Head Teacher's decisions shall not be called into question in any court of law.'

The Kent Free School ('Kent or KFS') has received many more applications than it has places, with three applicants for every available place. Hence, the Head Teacher has resolved to restrict offers of places to children who have at least obtained a level 5 grade in SATs and reside within a three-mile of the school.

Sue dwells in Oakfield with her ten-year-old son, Alex. Oakfield is a small village five miles from the KFS. Another local family has threatened Sue's family recently and Sue fears that Alex might be bullied or threatened by the children of this family if he attends the local village school. For this reason, Sue wishes to enrol Alex at Kent and his Health Visitor made a long statement detailing these exceptional social needs to support Sue's application. Alex obtained level 6 in his recent SATs.

Sue's application was rejected by Kent. In a letter from the Admissions Officer at Kent, Sue is told:

> Unfortunately, your application to Kent has been unsuccessful. Although we appreciate your family situation is troubling, we do not consider it a valid reason to offer your child a place here. Furthermore, your son only achieved level 4 in his SATs tests, which is below the minimum standard we seek on our path to become a centre of academic excellence. Most importantly, your distance from the school is outside our standard three-mile policy. Lastly, we must take note of the complaints we have received from parents regarding children from your village who have been allocated places.

**Please advise Alex and Sue under the procedural impropriety ground of judicial review claims.**

**Suggested Answer:**

Procedural ultra vires (PUV)

This is a statutory procedural requirement that is often encountered in an exam scenario, that is, for a decision maker to have a duty to give notice before a meeting/inquiry.

The word 'notice' is absent in our scenario and it is clear that Sue and Alex do not have a striking PUV argument here.

Section 1 states: 'When enrolling children, free schools should not be selective as regards academic ability.'

Sue and Alex could perhaps argue that this is a procedural requirement and that KFS's policy of only accepting applicants with at least a level 5 SATs result contravenes that procedural requirement. But in fact, is it a procedural requirement, or really a factor to be taken into account? Even if it was a procedural requirement, the presence of the word 'should' suggests that it is more of a suggestion or a guideline than a requirement.

Section 2 states: 'The distance of the school to a child's home is a factor that must be considered.'

In spite of the fact this section uses the word 'must' instead of 'should', Sue and Alex have no claim here, for in the unlikely event they could persuade the Administrative Court it is a procedural requirement rather than a factor to be taken into account, KFS did evaluate the distance of the school from Alex's home.

Section 3 states: 'A child's exceptional social needs may be worthy of consideration. To decide whether this is the case, evidence must be submitted by an independent qualified professional.'

Sue and Alex could claim this is a procedural requirement and that for the KFS to not take into consideration the Health Visitor's report on Alex's exceptional social needs violates that procedural requirement. However, the same question arises again: Is it a procedural requirement or a factor to be taken into account?

Even if it was accepted as a procedural requirement, the word 'may' suggests it is an option or guidance rather than a requirement.

In conclusion, **Sue and Alex's chances of success with this claim are almost non-existent**, as Sections 1 to 3 appear to cite factors to weigh up in reaching a decision rather than listing procedural requirements to be complied with prior to a decision being made.

### Duty Act Fairly: Natural Justice

### a-) The right to a fair hearing (RTAFH)

To be able to ascertain whether a claimant's RTAFH has been met, first of all we need to consider the amount that claimant forfeits, in that way we will be able to work out into which of Vice Chancellor Megarry's three categories - ***McInnes 1978*** - the claimant should go.

By this yardstick, Sue and Alex's claim for a violation of their RTAFH would not seem to be strong, as first and foremost Alex is in the first-time category – i.e. the lowest category with least to lose - because he is not forfeiting something he previously possessed. Alex is not a pupil at KFS and is applying to go there for the first time.

At first glance, Sue and Alex's RTAFH - *Fairmount 1976* - appears to have been met as:

**(i)** They knew the case against them (that KFS might reject Alex's application for a place at the school), and

**(ii)** They had the opportunity to reply (Sue applied to Kent for a place on Rueben's behalf and the Health Visitor submitted a statement detailing his exceptional social needs. Being allowed to present written arguments in their case would meet any fair hearing requirements for a first-time claimant).

The decisions in *Lloyd 1987, R (Smith and West) 2005* in which the HoL ruled that an oral hearing is in order for commercially important decisions. In the case of *Osborn 2013*, the Supreme Court indicated that the Judiciary is more likely to state a claimant deserved an oral hearing. In light of these cases, it is not at all likely that Sue and Alex would be able to convince the Administrative Court of their right to a full oral hearing including the opportunity to cross examine witnesses (as occurred in *Padfield 1968*), even if the decision to reject Alex's application was irrational. Please also note that *Lewis 1978* is met as the decision is final, not preliminary.

In conclusion, as a first-time claimant, **Alex has almost no chance of success with his RTAFH claim** as he was permitted to submit written reasons to back up his application and received several reasons in writing regarding why his application was rejected.

## b-) The right to be given reason(s)

Sue and Alex were provided with several written reasons. Hence, Sue and Alex could not expect to succeed with such a claim.

## c-) The rule against bias (RAB)

Sue and Alex have no grounds to claim a violation of the RAB. Hence, **Sue and Alex could not expect to succeed with such a claim.**

**2-)** The Minister for the Environment wrote to each local authority in England after the government was re-elected three years ago, following up an election manifesto pledge. The Minister reassured them that they had no grounds for concern over the development of green belt sites and that the government had no plans to reconsider that decision within the next five years. Kent Borough Council published this information on its official website.

However, only recently, the Minister for the Environment made public plans for the construction of 10,000 new homes in the Vale of Kent. In response, local residents have set up a campaign, the Kent NIMBY Alliance, to lead protests against the proposed development.

**Advise the Alliance on whether and how it may be able to challenge the above decision on the ground of legitimate expectation.**

### a-) Has a legitimate expectation arisen?

A representation made by a public body regarding its policy appears to be seen as amounting to a legitimate expectation. Consequently, the policy letter from the government would constitute the basis of a legitimate expectation.

This situation, the re-election of a government, is different to that in **Begbie 2000**, where the representation in question was made by a party in opposition, whose 'promise' was not deemed clear and unambiguous enough to be considered a legitimate expectation.

Judging by the evidence presented, it is a matter of debate whether the letter was clear and unambiguous **(IRC, ex p MFK 1990)**. Nowhere does it say that the government will not revisit the decision before 2016 (which might have been a fetter on its discretion), merely that it had 'no plans' to. Not having plans then does not mean absolutely that the government has ruled out, or is trying to rule out, the possibility that in the future (or, particularly, within the next five years) a plan might emerge. **Although the claim will probably fail here, you should still complete the remainder of the analysis.**

### b-) Was it lawful to have frustrated a legitimate expectation?

The promise in question was made to the whole country. In **Begbie 2000**, a promise had policy implications and was made on a 'macro' level, therefore, review was limited to a **Wednesbury** unreasonableness standard. Hence, when a decision is political or economic and has a general effect rather than one limited to a single group, the courts are unlikely to intervene with administrative autonomy. This principle would apply here.

The approach in macro-political or macro-economic matters is also applied in the updated Laws LJ. His method of proportionality is only used for decisions taken on a non-macro level.

Utilising the high threshold (or low intensity) test that will probably apply here, the Government will not find it hard to justify not keeping its promise (this would be the case even if the promise had been more clear-cut).

It is highly improbable that it would be seen as **Wednesbury** unreasonable for the Minister. He would be aware of having made a promise and of the consequences of breaking it, but will have decided to prioritise the wider public interest by permitting the building of new homes.

Consequently, the decision would probably be seen by the courts as something within the Executive's sphere of competence and only if the Minister had broken his promise in a bad faith (and/or had made a very clear promise – which was not the case) would a review of the decision **possibly have a chance of success.** A useful case to cite here (in the context of unreasonableness) would be **Nottinghamshire County Council 1986.**

# CHAPTER IX

## ADMINISTRATIVE JUSTICE: INQUIRIES, OMBUDSMAN AND TRIBUNALS

**Learning Outcomes:**

In this chapter, you should be able to understand:

- ✓ the importance, functions and types of public inquiry;
- ✓ the importance, functions and types of ombudsman;
- ✓ the tribunal system and its advantages and disadvantages.

**Questions and Answers:**

**1. What is a public inquiry?**

Public inquiries are significant investigations under the auspices of a government minister that can be granted special powers to ensure people testify and that other forms of evidence are disclosed. The only condition needed to justify a public inquiry is 'public concern' regarding a particular incident or series of incidents. Inquiries have dealt with all kinds of issues, from train accidents, fires, the mismanagement of pension funds, deaths in custody, outbreaks of disease, and the decision-making process culminating in going to war.[221]

Lord Howe, who has played different roles in several public inquiries, highlighted six functions, as follows:

- **Establishing the facts** providing a full and fair account of what happened, especially in circumstances where the facts are disputed, or the course and causation of events is not clear;
- **Learning from events** helping to prevent their recurrence by synthesising or distilling lessons which can be used to change practice;
- **Catharsis or therapeutic exposure** providing an opportunity for reconciliation and resolution, by bringing protagonists face to face with each other's perspectives and problems;
- **Reassurance** rebuilding public confidence after a major failure by showing that the government is making sure it is fully investigated and dealt with;

---

[221] Institute for Government, 'Public Inquiries', https://www.instituteforgovernment.org.uk/explainers/public-inquiries (accessed 30 July 2021).

- **Accountability, blame, and retribution** holding people and organisations to account, and sometimes indirectly contributing to the assignation of blame and to mechanisms for retribution;
- **Political considerations** serving a wider political agenda for government either in demonstrating that 'something is being done' or in providing leverage for change.[222]

## 2. Explain the types of public inquiry

There are two types of public inquiry:

**(i) Statutory public inquiries** function according to the rules in the Inquiries Act 2005 and Inquiry Rules 2006. These inquiries examine the details of ongoing inquiries under the Act and analyse the procedural issues inquiries face. For example, Grenfell and Blood Inquiry.

**(ii) Non-statutory inquiries** take place under the royal prerogative to establish a Royal Commission. Non-statutory inquiries are more flexible than statutory inquiries as regards determining an inquiry's procedures. This includes 'ad hoc' inquiries, such as the Chilcot Inquiry.

There are several main differences between statutory and non-statutory inquiries. Firstly, a non-statutory inquiry works with the voluntary compliance of witnesses. Secondly, it cannot take evidence on oath. Thirdly, statutory inquiries held under the Inquiries Act 2005 operate under a presumption that hearings will be public.[223]

## 3. How can an inquiry be established and what procedure will be used when conducting the inquiry? Is it acceptable that senior judges will often be asked to chair inquiries?

Inquiries Act 2005, Section 1(1) states a 'Minister'[224] may permit an inquiry to be held in relation to a case where it appears that

**(a)** particular incidents have led to, or may lead to, public concern, or

**(b)** where public concern exists regarding particular incidents.

---

[222] Howe, G., 'The management of public inquiries', *Political Quarterly* 70, (1999), pp. 294-304, summarised in Walsh, K. and Higgins, J., 'The use and impact of inquiries in the NHS', *British Medical Journal*, Vol 325, (2002), pp. 896-897; See also 'Select Committee on Public Administration First Report', https://publications.parliament.uk/pa/cm200405/cmselect/cmpubadm/51/5105.htm (accessed 30 July 2021).
[223] Cowie, G., 'Statutory commissions of inquiry: the Inquiries Act 2005', 8 July 2021, https://commonslibrary.parliament.uk/research-briefings/sn06410/ (accessed 30 July 2021).
[224] Section 1(2) explains who the Minister is: a UK, Scottish, Welsh and NI minister.

According to Section 3, the inquiry could be convened either by a single chairman, or by a chairman with more than one member.

Section 4 states that the inquiry panel will be appointed in the following way:

**(1)** Each member of an inquiry panel will be appointed by the Minister in writing.

**(2)** The instrument appointing the chairman must indicate that the inquiry is to be held under this Act.

**(3)** Prior to appointing a member to the inquiry panel (apart from the chairman) the Minister must engage in consultation with the person he has appointed, or intends to appoint, as chairman.

Section 10 regulates 'the appointment of a judge as panel member'. In other words, it is possible to appoint a senior judge as chair.

Note that proceedings may be held in public or in private, depending on the procedure appropriate for that particular inquiry.[225]

**4. What was the subject matter of recent public inquiries? What was the outcome of these inquiries?**

| Inquiry Name | Facts | Outcome |
| --- | --- | --- |
| **The Royal Commission on Tribunals of Inquiry (The Salmon Report)** | This report looked at the role of nurses in hospital management and the Cogwheel Report proposed specialty groupings of medical staff. | The report established 'six cardinal principles': 1. Prior to any person becoming involved in an inquiry, the Tribunal must be satisfied that the person is affected by issues the Tribunal is to investigate. 2. Before an individual involved in an inquiry is called to testify, the person should be told of any allegations against him and the facts of the evidence support these allegations. 3. (a) The witness should be granted the opportunity to prepare a case and to be assisted by legal advisers; (b) Legal expenses should in normal |

[225] LexisNexis, 'Public Inquiries', https://www.lexisnexis.co.uk/legal/guidance/public-inquiries (accessed 30 July 2021).

|  |  | circumstances come out of public funds. |
|---|---|---|
|  |  | 4. The person should be able to be examined by their own solicitor or counsel and to testify in public at the inquiry. |
|  |  | 5. Any material witness called at the inquiry should be heard, if reasonably practicable. |
|  |  | 6. The person should be able to benefit from cross-examination carried out by their own solicitor or counsel of any evidence which may affect them.[226] |
| **The Iraq Inquiry** | The Iraq Inquiry (also known as the Chilcot Inquiry) was a British public inquiry into the UK's role in the Iraq War. | The report concluded that Mr Blair had exaggerated his influence on US decisions on Iraq; and the UK's relationship with the US does not necessitate unconditional support.<br><br>It stressed the importance of ministerial discussion encouraging open and informed debate. It also emphasised the importance of making sure civilian and military arms of government have the right equipment.<br><br>In future, all facets of any intervention must to be calculated and rigorously discussed. Decisions taken need to be fully implemented.[227] |
| **The Leveson Inquiry** | The Leveson inquiry was a judicial public inquiry which examined the prevalent culture, practices and ethics in the British newspaper industry after the News International phone-hacking scandal. | It probed the existing culture and ethics of the British media, recommending a new, independent body replace the Press Complaints Commission. Such a body would need to be created by Parliament enacting new laws. Leveson concluded |

---

[226] Report of the Royal Commission on Tribunals of Inquiry, Cmnd 3121, November 1966.
[227] 'The Report of the Iraq Inquiry', July 2016, https://assets.publishing.service.gov.uk/government/uploads/system/uploads/attachment_data/file/535407/The_Report_of_the_Iraq_Inquiry_-_Executive_Summary.pdf (accessed 30 July 2021).

| | | |
|---|---|---|
| | | that the existing Press Complaints Commission was inadequate, and proposed that a new independent body, would have sanctions at its disposal, including fines and stipulating more prominent apologies and corrections.[228] |
| **The Grenfell Tower Inquiry** | The Grenfell Tower Inquiry was set up to examine the background of and incidents that took place during the fire at Grenfell Tower on the night of 14 June 2017. | The Chairman published his Phase 1 report on 30 October 2019. |
| | | In the Phase 1 report the following recommendations were made: |
| | | 1. A law should be enacted requiring owners and managers of high-rise residential buildings to give information about external wall materials and building plans to their local fire and rescue service. |
| | | 2. Inspections by the Fire Brigade of high-rise buildings to be improved and better training to be provided to crews to carry out more thorough risk evaluations. Lifts used by fire fighters need more regular inspections. |
| | | 3. There must be better communications between fire brigade control rooms and incident commanders and a dedicated communication link must be introduced to provide this. |
| | | 4. Government should introduce national guidelines for implementing partial or total evacuations of high-rise residential buildings. |

[228] 'An Inquiry into the Culture, Practices and Ethics of the Press', November 2012, https://assets. publishing.service.gov.uk/government/uploads/system/uploads/attachment_data/file/ 229039/ 0779.pdf (accessed 30 July 2021).

| | | 5. Fire doors in all such residential properties should inspected as a matter of urgency. |
| | | 6. Data links provided by helicopters of the National Police Air Service should be improved, as pictures sent on the night of the Grenfell fire could not be viewed by the London Fire Brigade because the encryption was incompatible with its receiving equipment. |
| | | Phase 2 of the Inquiry is exploring the causes of these incidents, including how the Grenfell Tower was in a condition that allowed the fire to spread rapidly, as identified by the Phase 1 report. The Phase 2 report had yet to be published at the time this book was written.[229] |
| **The Infected Blood Inquiry** | This independent public statutory inquiry was established to examine how men, women and children treated by the NHS have received infected blood and infected blood products since 1970. | At the time of writing, this inquiry report had yet to be published.[230] |

## 5. Are an inquiry's recommendations enforceable?

An inquiry's recommendations are not legally binding. It is for the government or other public bodies to implement any recommendations. But the Government generally indicates which recommendations will be accepted.

It is important to note that inquiries cannot replace existing legal procedures. Any criminal proceedings would usually take place before an inquiry.[231]

---

[229] 'Grenfell Tower Inquiry: Phase 1 Report Overview', June 2017, https://assets.grenfelltowerinquiry.org.uk/GTI%20-%20Phase%201%20report%20Executive%20Summary.pdf (accessed 30 July 2021).

[230] 'Infected Blood Inquiry', https://www.infectedbloodinquiry.org.uk/ (accessed 30 July 2021).

[231] Cabinet Office, 'Inquiries Guidance: Guidance for Inquiry Chairs and Secretaries, and Sponsor Departments', https://www.parliament.uk/globalassets/documents/lords-committees/Inquiries-Act-2005/caboffguide.pdf (accessed 30 July 2021).

## 6. What is the Ombudsman?

An ombudsman is an independent and impartial person who is appointed to examine complaints relating to companies and organisations.

You can take a complaint to an ombudsman if you have already complained to an organisation and your problem was not resolved by the company's complaints procedure. An ombudsman will also get involved if the organisation takes too long to resolve your complaint. This is usually eight weeks, but it depends on the scheme in use.

An ombudsman will not become involved in your case if you have already commenced court action.[232]

## 7. Explain the types of ombudsman

There are two types of ombudsman:[233]

### Private sector ombudsman

These ombudsman deal with financial and consumer complaints. Private sector ombudsman include:

- Energy deals with complaints about gas and electricity companies;
- Communications and CISAS assist with complaints relating to phone and internet providers;
- The Motor Ombudsman deals with complaints about sales, service or repairs of vehicles;
- The Rail Ombudsman deals with complaints concerning train companies;
- The Financial Ombudsman Service resolves problems customers experience with banks, insurance, payment protection insurance, loans, mortgages, pensions and deals with other financial complaints;
- The Property Ombudsman and the Property Redress Scheme sort out disputes between consumers and property agents;
- The Furniture Ombudsman can resolve problems with furniture and other retail purchases and home improvements;
- The Pensions Ombudsman examines complaints relating to pension schemes and decisions made by the Pension Protection Fund and the Financial Assistance Scheme - they cannot deal with complaints about the State Pension;

---

[232] Citizen Advice Bureau, 'Complaining to an ombudsman', https://www.citizensadvice.org.uk/consumer/get-more-help/how-to-use-an-ombudsman-in-england/#:~:text=An%20ombudsman%20is%20a%20person,you%20complain%20to%20an%20ombudsman (accessed 30 July 2021).
[233] Ibid.

- The Legal Ombudsman can assist in resolving legal service disputes.

## Public sector ombudsman

They chiefly examine complaints relating to government organisations and public services. These include:

- The Parliamentary and Health Service Ombudsman looks into complaints about government departments and some other public bodies. They can also examine complaints about NHS hospitals or community health services;
- The Local Government and Social Care Ombudsman examines complaints made about local councils, care homes and certain other organisations that provide local public services;
- The Housing Ombudsman can assist you if you are a tenant or leaseholder and you are involved in a dispute with your landlord, as long as they are a social landlord or a voluntary member of their scheme;
- The Prisons and Probation Ombudsman investigates deaths and complaints regarding incidents in custody;
- The European Ombudsman deals with complaints concerning institutions of the European Union.

## 8. What sanctions can the Ombudsman impose?

After looking at evidence from both sides, the ombudsman will reach a decision. Such investigations can be time-consuming, so a decision may take some time to be reached.

If the ombudsman finds your complaint to be justified, s/he will make a recommendation as to what the organisation should do to remedy the situation.

A public sector ombudsman has no power to coerce an organisation to comply with the recommendations, but organisations in most instances do so.

The decision of a private sector ombudsman could be legally binding and would be of a standard that you might not obtain in a court. For instance, the ombudsman might ask the organisation to apologise or order it to compensate you if you have been left out of pocket.[234]

---

[234] Ibid.

## 9. What are the benefits of the Ombudsman service?

**Advantages**:

- No expense incurred;
- Independent from government;
- Reports relating to systematic issues in an agency or to the rollout of a government programme may be published;
- Bad practices may be remedied;
- Private sector ombudsman's decisions are legally binding;
- Ombudsman can recommend conciliation in addition to investigation.

Disadvantages:

- Do not offer rapid solution to complex problems;
- Complainant has no say in the investigation. That is, the Ombudsman does not represent the complainant solely, and they have the right to refuse to address a specific matter;
- Decisions of Public Sector Ombudsman are not binding.[235]

## 10. Briefly outline how the tribunal works and describe the advantages and disadvantages of the system in relation to ordinary courts.

A tribunal, similar to a court of law, is a forum at which contentious issues are settled by an impartial adjudicator. A network of tribunals, each one concentrating on a specific field of law, is part of the civil justice system and also a significant element of administrative law. There are tribunals that deal with Agriculture, Aviation, Data Protection, Education, Employment, Fair Trading, Financial Services, Foreign Compensation, Immigration, Land, Taxation, Misuse of Drugs, National Health Service, Pensions, and Rents.[236]

People who go to tribunals often do not have legal representation. Consequently, judges and members usually explain how the tribunal functions and ask questions to participants in order to obtain more information regarding the case in question.[237]

---

[235] Legal Services Commission of South Australia, 'Advantages and disadvantages of using the Ombudsman', 30 July 2012, https://lawhandbook.sa.gov.au/ch09s01s02s03.phpd (accessed 30 July 2020).
[236] Barnett, p. 663-664; Clements, pp. 209-224.
[237] Courts and Tribunals Judiciary, 'Tribunals', https://www.judiciary.uk/you-and-the-judiciary/going-to-court/tribunals/ (accessed 30 July 2021).

If the decision made by the judge in your case is not the one you were expecting, it may be possible to appeal to a judge in a higher court, or in tribunal cases to the Upper Tribunal or Employment Appeal Tribunal.[238]

## 11. What are the advantages and disadvantages of a tribunal system?

There are several advantages and disadvantages:[239]

| ADVANTAGES | DISADVANTAGES |
|---|---|
| • They are legally binding, but the process is less formal and fair;<br>• Cheaper;<br>• Quicker;<br>• Lay members examine the case alongside the tribunal judge;<br>• They are not confined by the rigidity of precedent, and have more discretionary powers at their disposal;<br>• Independent, similar to courts. | • Delay may occur on account of case being complex, and there may be a wait for a case hearing;<br>• Public funding does not cover all costs;<br>• The procedure is quite formal and may be difficult for individuals who represent themselves;<br>• Right of appeal is often limited;<br>• Experts are not always unbiased;<br>• No precedent, so decisions may be unpredictable;<br>• Parties may feel intimidated regarding taking a case to court, particularly without a legal representative. |

## A SAMPLE ESSAY QUESTION:

"In recent years, access to justice has been greatly compromised in England and Wales."

**Explain what is meant by 'access to justice' and why it is important.**

**Evaluate whether there are viable alternatives for obtaining legal advice following the cuts to legal aid.**

**Suggested Answer:**

### Introduction

You should make a short summary of what access to justice means and explain the changes to legal aid introduced by the Legal Aid, Sentencing and Punishment of Offenders Act in order to reduce the costs to the Exchequer.[240]

---

[238] Courts and Tribunals Judiciary, 'Appeals Process', https://www.judiciary.uk/you-and-the-judiciary/appeals-process/ (accessed 30 July 2021).

[239] Get revising, 'Tribunals', https://getrevising.co.uk/grids/tribunals (accessed 30 July 2021).

[240] The Legal Aid, Sentencing and Punishment of Offenders Act became law in May 2012 and came into effect in April 2013.

**The main body**

**Firstly, you should explain the significance of 'Access to Justice':**

Access to justice relates to access to legal advice and/or representation when dealing with a specific issue or dispute.

It is absolutely fundamental because legal questions are usually complex and can have consequences that affect an individual's freedom, financial situation and reputation. Therefore, cases need the input of experts or specialists to address these issues properly and efficiently. If people try to represent themselves, they may not have the knowledge and skills requires and only make things worse.

Therefore, Article 6(1) of HRA/ECHR safeguards the right to a fair trial, stating "In the determination of his civil rights and obligations or of any criminal charge against him, everyone is entitled to a fair and public hearing within a reasonable time by an independent and impartial tribunal established by law..."

**Secondly, you should explain the Legal Aid Scheme in the UK:**

In order to help people, access to justice in the UK, the Legal Aid scheme was launched in 1949. To obtain legal aid, an individual generally has to prove they cannot afford to meet legal costs by providing details and evidence of income, benefits, savings and property, including that of their partner. The issue in question also must be serious. If the applicant is under 18, they may have to provide information regarding the income of their parents or guardians.[241]

The Legal Aid Agency is an executive agency of the Ministry of Justice which deals with civil legal aid in England and Wales. The Agency's objectives are as follows:

- Provide simple, timely and reliable access to legal aid;
- Build strong relationships across Government and the justice system;
- Secure value for money for the taxpayer in all that we do;
- Achieve our full potential through being fair, proud and supportive.[242]

In addition to the Legal Aid Agency, there are other alternative sources in the UK, such as Citizen Advice Bureaus, law centres and pro bono which can be used to gain access to civil justice. Or, alternatively, you can use your own

---

[241] 'Legal Aid', https://www.gov.uk/legal-aid/eligibility (accessed 30 July 2021).
[242] Legal Aid Agency, 'Annual Report and Accounts 2019-20', https://assets.publishing.service.gov.uk/government/uploads/system/uploads/attachment_data/file/902746/Legal_Aid_Agency_annual_report_and_accounts_2019_to_2020.pdf (accessed 30 July 2021).

resources such as insurance funding, conditional fee agreements and damage-based agreements to access to justice.

The legal aid budget has been reduced by around £350 million per year since the introduction of legal aid reforms.[243] As part of these reforms, the fees received by lawyers for legal aid work were reduced, eligibility requirements were tightened and legal aid is no longer available for family law matters, debt, housing, employment and social welfare. Since 2000, there have been cuts in legal aid for cases of personal injury and domestic violence.

Cuts have had a major impact in several areas. The Constitutional Affairs Select Committee published a report on the Carter Review of Legal Aid (May 2007):

- Lawyers are unable to make a career in this area of law;
- There is no incentive to address complex/substantial areas of law – limited profitability means more defendants have no representation – hence increased risk of serious miscarriages of justice;
- Standard of legal advice has dropped.[244]

**Finally, you should elaborate as to whether the changes are or are not sufficient and effective:**

On the one hand, you can present the case arguing that changes are not sufficient and effective:

- Shortage of lawyers to do legal aid case work on account of cuts in funding and restrictions on fees charged and tendering for legal aid work.
- Rural communities have difficulty obtaining legal aid locally due to point 1.
- Standard of legal advice will fall if there are fewer lawyers doing legal aid work. Good lawyers will be put off considering legal aid work.
- More litigants representing themselves or using a friend will lead to delays in trials.
- Vulnerable people, like children, will find it difficult to access advice.[245]
- Violation of the right to a fair trial under Article 6 of HRA/ECHR.

---

[243] Andersson, J., 'Legal Aid Fee Cuts To Evidence Work Have Been Declared Unlawful', 3 August 2018, https://eachother.org.uk/legal-aid-fee-cuts-to-evidence-work-have-been-declared-unlawful/#:~:text=The%20Legal%20Aid%2C%20Sentencing%20and,aid%20budget%20since%20that%20year (accessed 30 July 2021).

[244] Select Committee on Constitutional Affairs Third Report, 'Recommendations', https://publications.parliament.uk/pa/cm200607/cmselect/cmconst/223/22313.htm (accessed 30 July 2021).

[245] Bowcott, O., 'Children being denied justice by legal cuts, says children's commissioner', The Guardian, 24 September 2014, http://www.theguardian.com/law/2014/sep/24/children-denied-justice-legal-cuts-children-commissioner (accessed 30 July 2021).

- The rule of law that everyone is equal before the law is under threat as only the wealthy will have access to high quality legal advice.
- Problems in accessing legal aid in cases of domestic violence.
- The balancing of guilty and not-guilty pleas will result in there being more guilty pleas as barristers will earn the same fee for ending a trial early on a guilty plea as they will going to full trial.
- Recommendations to link court fees in monetary claims to 5% of the value of the claim (over £10,000) will make people less willing to go to court.

On the other hand, you can elaborate the case arguing that changes are sufficient and effective:

- Cuts to legal aid are necessary as the current system is unsustainable in the long-term. The Government currently spends around £2 billion a year on legal aid. This will be cut to £1.5 billion.
- The reduction will enable the Government to save taxpayers' money.
- According to the Council of Europe, England and Wales were the third highest among forty-eight countries to spend on legal aid in 2018.[246]
- Eligibility requirements for legal aid ensure that only people who really need legal aid have access to it. The rights of the poorest in society are safeguarded.

## Conclusion

You can then come to a brief conclusion. Ideally, you will briefly summarise what you have already discussed in the main body. And then, in the next paragraph, you should explain what you think in light of the arguments stated above.

---

[246] Council of Europe European Commission for the efficiency of justice, 'European judicial systems CEPEJ Evaluation Report 2020 Evaluation cycle (2018 data)', Council of Europe, 2020, https://rm.coe.int/evaluation-report-part-1-english/16809fc058 (accessed 30 July 2021); See also Barrett, D., 'UK is named the legal aid capital of Europe as our spending dwarfs almost every nation on the continent', The Daily Mail, 23 October 2020, https://www.dailymail.co.uk/news/article-8870543/UK-named-legal-aid-capital-Europe.html (accessed 30 July 2021).

# SUMMARY: SAMPLE TEST QUESTIONS

## PART A - CONSTITUTIONAL LAW

**1) Which one of the following describes the United Kingdom's constitution?**
  a) An absolute monarchy
  b) A federal state
  c) A constitutional monarchy
  d) A republic

**2) Constitutions may be in the form of a codified or an uncodified. Which of the answers below is CORRECT for the United Kingdom?**
  a) Although the United Kingdom does not have a written constitution, it does have recourse to a Constitutional Court with the power to annul Acts of Parliament.
  b) A codified constitution does not exist in the United Kingdom. No individual document oversees the way in which the state functions.
  c) The United Kingdom constitution is codified and is made up of several documents.
  d) The United Kingdom constitution consists of a single written document.

**3) Which one of the following sources is NOT the United Kingdom's constitution?**
  a) Customs
  b) Conventions
  c) Case law
  d) European Union Treaties

**4) Prerogative powers**
  a) restrict parliamentary sovereignty.
  b) are superior to legislation.
  c) are exempt from any form of judicial review.
  d) may be abolished by Parliament.

**5) Which one of the following best describes the legal role of the Monarch in the legislative process?**
  a) The Monarch usually gives Royal Assent as a matter of convention.
  b) The Monarch writes the laws of the United Kingdom.
  c) The Monarch must always give Royal Assent so legislation is enacted.
  d) The Monarch's role in the legislative process is ceremonial.

151

**6) How many of the following statements are CORRECT?**

(i)   The Prime Minister is appointed by the Monarch.

(ii)  The Prime Minister may be a member of the House of Lords.

(iii) The Prime Minister must not be an MP.

(iv)  The Prime Minister is not elected.

a) None          b) One           c) Two          d) Three

**7) Of the options below, which one most accurately describes the perception of parliamentary sovereignty contained in the United Kingdom constitution?**

a) Parliament is free to legislate in any way it feels is right.

b) If it is of a mind to do so, Parliament may remove the Monarch and appoint a new one.

c) Parliament is not allowed to enact legislation that contradicts European Union Law.

d) Parliament has an obligation to operate within the European Convention on Human Rights.

**8) Which one of the following statements concerning the primary role of the House of Commons is CORRECT?**

a) The role of the House of Commons is to act as the second legislative chamber of the United Kingdom.

b) The main function of the House of Commons is to supply all the personnel who constitute the government.

c) The role of the House of Commons is to serve the nations that make up the United Kingdom.

d) The House of Commons is the chamber of the United Kingdom Parliament that is publicly elected at a General Election.

**9) Most Peers in the House of Lords are:**

a) Hereditary

b) Elected

c) Nominated

d) Judges

**10) Which one of the following statements is CORRECT?**

a) The European Communities Act 1972 may only be repealed if the European Union agrees.

b) The Scotland Act 1998 can only be repealed by the Scottish Parliament.

c) The Parliament Act 1911 is inviolate, meaning it cannot be abrogated.

d) The three formulations above are all wrong.

**11) Which one of the following best describes the important legal principle of *Entick v Carrington 1765*?**
 a) The courts will strike down all warrants that are not issued by judges.
 b) The government can validly seize property in times of national emergency.
 c) Executive actions must be premised upon a legal basis. If they are not, they are not legally valid.
 d) Warrants are not a known device of the United Kingdom legal system.

**12) The electoral system used in UK General Elections (known as First Past the Post) generally leads to:**
 a) Certain constituencies not electing an MP.
 b) A government established by a political party with an absolute majority of seats in the House of Commons.
 c) A situation where no party has a majority of MPs, called a 'hung' Parliament.
 d) A government consisting of a coalition of two or more parties.

**13) The separation of powers is made up of three branches:**
 a) The Queen, Executive and Legislative
 b) The Queen, Legislative and Judiciary
 c) Legislative, Judiciary and People
 d) Executive, Legislative and Judiciary

**14) Which of the following statements about the Rule of Law are INCORRECT?**
 a) Everybody equals before law.
 b) There should be no higher law other than rights of individuals.
 c) Regular law is supreme over arbitrary power.
 d) Parliament is supreme law-making body and may enact or repeal laws on any subject.

**15) Which one is the following statements Dicey's version of rule of law includes?**
 a) No one is above the law.
 b) The rule of law is entrenched.
 c) The rule of law means respect for fundamental human rights.
 d) The prime minister is not subject to the rule of law.

**16) Which of the following statements about the Parliamentary Supremacy are INCORRECT?**

a) Regular law is supreme over arbitrary power.

b) Each Parliament has authority to legislate, and is not restricted by a previous parliament. In the same way it cannot bind a future parliament.

c) The validity of an Act of Parliament cannot be challenged by any other person or institution.

d) Parliament is the paramount legislative body and has the power to introduce or repeal any laws it wishes.

**17) Which one of the following describes the power of the courts in relation to constitutional conventions?**

a) The courts can identify but not enforce conventions.

b) Conventions are not laws and are therefore irrelevant to the courts.

c) The courts have no jurisdiction over conventions.

d) There are some conventions the courts cannot rule on because of their subject matter.

**18) Cabinet collective responsibility means:**

a) Cabinet has to express a uniform view.

b) Debate in Cabinet is confidential.

c) Neither A or B.

d) Both A and B.

**19) Of the following statements, which best describes delegated legislation?**

a) A law introduced by a person or body outside Parliament, although authorised by Parliament.

b) Legislation created by a person or body outside Parliament that only relates to protection of the environment.

c) A law introduced by a person or body outside Parliament, based on powers granted by the Privy Council.

d) Legislation enacted by a person or body outside Parliament through a particular form of constitutional Act initiated in a national crisis.

**20) Which of these statements are accurate? (More than one option may be selected)**

a) The Standing Committee stage follows the second reading.

b) A bill may be introduced to either the House of Commons or the House of Lords.

c) The first reading is just a formal stage where only the title of the bill is read out.

d) A bill can only be set in motion in the House of Commons.

**21) Which of the statements below best describes the objective of the second reading of a bill?**

    a) It is a chance for Parliament to debate changes that occurred at the Committee stage.

    b) It is a chance for Parliament to debate the main principal of a bill.

    c) It is a time when Parliament can debate a bill in detail.

    d) It is a time when Parliament can debate amendments added to the bill by the other chamber.

**22) Which Act established the Supreme Court?**

    a) The Constitutional Reform Act 2005

    b) The Courts Act 2009

    c) The Supreme Court Act 2009

    d) The Constitutional Reform Act 2009

**23) What are the mechanisms NOT for scrutinising Government?**

    a) European Union Parliament

    b) Judicial review

    c) Select committees

    d) Debates

**24) What are NOT the internal threats against Parliamentary Supremacy?**

    a) Devolution

    b) 'Manner and form' entrenchment

    c) Implied repeal/constitutional statutes

    d) European Convention on Human Rights

**25) What is 'devolution'?**

    a) Efforts to stop a revolution.

    b) The transfer of power from central government to regional government.

    c) It has the opposite meaning to evolution.

    d) It signifies the end of a parliament when a general election is declared.

## PART B – HUMAN RIGHTS

**1) Which one of the following statements about the Human Rights Act 1998 is CORRECT?**
a) The Act was cited as a 'constitutional statute' in ***Thoburn v Sunderland City Council***.
b) There was a need for such an Act to implement European Union law in the United Kingdom.
c) The Act is inviolate and cannot be repealed.
d) The Act imposes an obligation on UK courts to consider European Union law when reaching judgments.

**2) Which one of the following most accurately describes the power of the courts under section 4 of the Human Rights Act 1998?**
a) Primary legislation may be declared illegal.
b) Primary legislation may be rewritten to give it a new meaning.
c) Primary legislation may be disapplied.
d) Primary legislation may be declared incompatible.

**3) Which one of the following best describes the relationship of the European Court of Human Rights to domestic courts?**
a) Domestic courts must take into account any Court judgments in accordance with the Human Rights Act 1998.
b) The Court has the power to override domestic law.
c) The Court can quash judgments made by domestic courts.
d) The European Court of Human Rights has the status of being the highest court of the United Kingdom.

**4) Which one of the four options below describes the kind of action entailed when a celebrity brings a case under Article 8 of the European Convention on Human Rights against a newspaper?**
a) As newspapers are public authorities, it is a horizontal action.
b) As newspapers are public authorities, it is a vertical action.
c) It is just a private law claim.

**Since a newspaper is not a public authority, it is a horizontal action.**

**5) How many of the following statements about the case of A & Others v Secretary of state for the Home Department are INCORRECT?**

   **(i)**   The case set the precedent that detention without trial is legal in the event of there being an existential threat to the nation.

   **(ii)**   The case set the precedent that judges may override the authority of Parliament if human rights are at stake.

   **(iii)**   The case set the standard that courts have jurisdiction in human rights cases.

   **(iv)**   The case set the precedent that judges will always allow the executive to decide on matters of national security.

a) One      b) Two      c) Three      d) All Four

**6) The European Convention on Human Rights was drawn up by the ...**
a)  Council of Europe
b)  Council of Members
c)  European Council
d)  European Commission

**7) Read the following sentence and select the correct answers from those listed in A – D.**

Prior to the ____[1]_____ of the Human Rights Act 1998, individuals in England and Wales wanting to enforce their Convention rights had to travel to the _____[2]_____ located in ____[3]____ to have their case heard.
a)  [1] coming into force [2] European Court of Justice [3] Brussels
b)  [1] enactment [2] European Court of Human Rights [3] Strasbourg
c)  [1] coming into force [2] European Court of Human Rights [3] Strasbourg
d)  [1] enactment [2] European Court of Justice [3] Strasbourg

**8) Courts have the power to declare that a provision of primary legislation contravenes the European Convention on Human Rights. What is the outcome of such a declaration?**
a)  It notifies the government that the provision is not 'Convention compliant' and ends the use of the provision.
b)  The primary legislation in question is repealed.
c)  It informs the government that the provision contravenes the Convention, but the provision continues to be used.
d)  It amends the provision at issue.

**9) What general principles does the European Court of Human Rights follow to delineate the boundaries of state liability and individual rights?**
   a)  Margin of appreciation, proportionality and equity
   b)  Margin of appreciation and equity
   c)  Equitable principles
   d)  Margin of appreciation, proportionality and positive/negative obligations

**10) According to the Police and Criminal Evidence Act 1984, what is the maximum total time an individual may be held for questioning?**
   a)  36 hours
   b)  48 hours
   c)  72 hours
   d)  96 hours

**11) What is the time period a person may be restricted to access his/her solicitor under Schedule 8 of the Anti-Terrorism Act 2000 and Code H of the Police and Criminal Evidence Act 1984?**
   a)  36 hours
   b)  48 hours
   c)  72 hours
   d)  96 hours

**12) In *McCann, Farrell & Savage v United Kingdom* the Court concluded there had been a breach of Article 2 of the European Convention on Human Rights because:**
   a)  The three people had been killed with an implementation of force which could not be deemed 'absolutely necessary'.
   b)  The utilisation of force to intentionally kill a person is permitted in the United Kingdom.
   c)  The employment of force was not sufficient given the conditions in which the three terrorists were found.
   d)  The policy of 'shoot-to-kill' was not considered appropriate to the definition of national security.

**13) If a consistent interpretation of rights embodied in the European Convention on Human Rights is not feasible under Section 3 of the Human Rights Act 1998, the judiciary may:**
   a)  Allow a torts claim for damages against the State.
   b)  Not take any action, as the Act does not empower them to do so.
   c)  Declare that the provisions are incompatible.
   d)  Disregard the Act in question.

**14) Which part of the Human Rights Act 1998 obliges domestic courts to take into account judgments of the European Court of Human Rights?**
   a) Section 19
   b) Section 3
   c) Section 2
   d) Section 1

**15) Which of the following of the European Convention on Human Rights is an absolute right?**
   a) Article 8
   b) Article 3
   c) Article 6
   d) Article 9

**16) As the United Kingdom is no longer a member of the European Union, the European Convention on Human Rights:**
   a) is still applicable.
   b) has been repealed.
   c) does not require consideration by UK courts.
   d) is no longer relevant.

**17) Of the formulations below, which one is the best explanation of the constitutional importance of freedom of expression?**
   a) Freedom of expression is an absolutely vital element of pluralism, tolerance and broadmindedness, pillars of a 'democratic society'.
   b) Freedom of expression is not conducive to the development of social networks in the private sector.
   c) Freedom of expression is not a concept that encourages inclusion and diversity.
   d) In a constitutional system freedom of expression is not important.

**18) Which one of the following is NOT a preliminary requirement in human rights cases in the UK?**
   a) Amenability
   b) Jurisdiction
   c) Standing
   d) Ouster Clause

**19) Core public authorities are always subject to section 6(1) in respect of all of their acts, whereas hybrid public authorities are only subject to section 6(1) in respect of those of its acts which are deemed to be of a public function.**
   a) Correct          b) Incorrect

**20) Which one of the following is NOT a type of victim?**
a) Potential
b) Indirect
c) Direct
d) Partial

**21) Which of the following bodies would be considered hybrid public authorities?**
a) The Police
b) The Army
c) Housing Association
d) City Council

**22) What does NOT Article 3 cover?**
a) Torture
b) Degrading punishment
c) Inhuman treatment
d) Slavery

**23) The first paragraph of Article 6 applies to both civil and criminal proceedings, but the second and third paragraphs apply only to criminal proceedings.**
a) Correct
b) Incorrect

**24) Which one of the legitimate aims is exclusively stated in Article 8(2)?**
a) Public safety
b) The protection of health
c) The economic well-being of the country
d) The protection of the rights and freedoms of others

**25) Which article is NOT stated in Article 15 as a non-derogable right?**
a) Article 3
b) Article 4 (paragraph 1)
c) Article 7
d) Article 10

## PART C – ADMINISTRATIVE LAW

**1) Which of the formulations below come within the ambit of Judicial Review?**

a) The accountability the government has for accidental damage or personal injury that occurs on government property.

b) A private organisation's contractual accountability.

c) The wielding of a power granted to a public body by statute or case law.

d) Matters relating to employment disagreements between public servants and the Government.

**2) Which of the below is NOT a judicial review preliminary requirement?**

a) Amenability

b) Standing

c) Procedural exclusivity

d) Legitimate expectation

**3) Of the options below, which best describes the test for amenability to judicial review established in *ex parte Datafin?***

a) If a public institution was acting in an ineffective manner, would the private sector create an entity to meet the need?

b) If there were no publicly created institution, would the private sector create an entity to perform the role?

c) If there were no publicly created institution, would the government set one up?

d) If there were not a privately run entity, would the government intervene and set up a body to perform the role?

**4) Regarding the rules on standing relating to judicial review, which one of the options below should be considered relevant when standing for groups is the issue at hand?**

a) The group's available funding.

b) The membership of the group's age.

c) The membership of the group's level of education.

d) The group's knowledge, expertise and resources in the subject in question.

161

**5) Which one of the following is an important case on standing for judicial review?**

    a)  Ex parte Fleet Street Casuals

    b)  GCHQ

    c)  R v A (Complainants Sexual History)

    d)  O'Reilly v Mackmann

**6) Of the options below, which best explains the definition of standing as regards judicial review?**

    a)  Standing explains if a group or individual is in a position to make a claim for judicial review.

    b)  Standing explains whether judicial review should be embarked upon instead of private law.

    c)  Standing is a type of test for a victim subjected to judicial review.

    d)  Standing implies that a person or a group as a victim is in a good position to make a claim.

**7) Which of the following is NOT a ground under judicial review?**

    a)  Illegality

    b)  Irrationality

    c)  Breach of contract

    d)  Procedural impropriety

**8) Which of the below subcategories is NOT part of the ground of illegality?**

    a)  Error of law

    b)  Error of fact

    c)  Ultra vires

    d)  Legitimate expectation

**9) Which of the statements below regarding the decision in *GCHQ* is INCORRECT?**

    a)  The Council for Civil Service Unions received standing to bring a claim for judicial review.

    b)  Concerns relating to national security hindered the legitimate expectations of the Council for Civil Service Unions.

    c)  Exercise of RPP by a PM is protected from judicial review.

    d)  Exercise of RPP by a PM is not protected from judicial review. The list established by Lord Roskill of non- justiciable prerogatives was only deemed an observation.

**10) James applies to his local council for a licence to drive a taxi. He knows that all other applicants have been granted an interview and chance to make oral presentations before a determination is made. He is denied an interview and refused a licence.**

**Which one of the following is the most likely subcategory James would raise?**

a) Error of law
b) Error of fact
c) Legitimate expectation
d) Improper purpose

**11) Which one of the following describes the legal principle established by *Wednesbury Corporation*?**

a) A decision that is illegal is void.
b) A decision that is unreasonable is void.
c) A decision that is so unreasonable that no other decision-maker could have reached it, can be quashed.
d) Decisions that are disproportionate can be quashed.

**12) In *CCSU v Minister for the Civil Service* [1985] AC 374, Lord Diplock defined 'irrationality' as:**

a) Any kind of court decision.
b) Irrationality does not exist as a concept in judicial decision-making.
c) A decision considered to be disgraceful by the defendant because it outrageous in its defiance of logic.
d) A decision which is so outrageous in its defiance of logic that no sensible person who had applied his mind to the question to be decided could have arrived at it.

**13) Which one of the following is a subcategory of unreasonableness?**

a) Errors of fact
b) Improper purpose
c) Irrelevant considerations
d) Oppressive decisions

**14) Which one of the following best describes the outcome of *Ex Parte Pinochet*?**

a) Bias can never be pecuniary.
b) Bias must be pecuniary.
c) Biased decision makers do not automatically make biased decisions.
d) Bias may be non-pecuniary.

**15) Which one of the following is NOT a factor of procedural ultra vires?**

    a)  The wording in the enabling Act

    b)  The importance of oppressive decisions

    c)  The severity of the consequences for the claimant

    d)  The degree of effort the decision maker has made to comply

**16) Which one of the following two types of decision would attract the higher duty of fairness?**

    a)  Application for a planning permission.

    b)  A decision involving fundamental human rights.

    c)  Application for a compulsory purchase order.

    d)  Application for a licence.

**17) Which one of the following statements concerning fairness is CORRECT?**

    a)  Fairness is a duty in decisions, both of judicial and administrative.

    b)  Fairness is only a requirement in judicial decisions.

    c)  Fairness is usually not a duty in common law, when it is required by statute.

    d)  Fairness is never a requirement in administrative decisions.

**18) Which one of the following is a subcategory of legitimate expectation?**

    a)  Promise based

    b)  Prospective

    c)  Historical

    d)  Rights based

**19) Which of the below better defines 'procedural impropriety'?**

    a)  Excess of jurisdiction

    b)  Improper purpose

    c)  The use by barristers of improper language in Court

    d)  A non-observance of the basic rules of natural justice

**20) Which of the below subcategories is NOT part of the ground of procedural impropriety?**

    a)  Oppressive decisions

    b)  Procedural ultra vires

    c)  The rule against bias

    d)  The right to fair hearing

**21) Which of the below subcategories is NOT part of the ground of unreasonableness/irrationality?**
- a) Oppressive decisions
- b) Bias
- c) Material defects in a decision-making process
- d) Arbitrary violation of constitutional principles

**22) Which of the following are mechanism of Alternative Administrative Justice apart from judicial review:**
- **(i)** Tribunal
- **(ii)** Inquires
- **(iii)** Ombudsmen
- **(iv)** A civil claim

- a) i, ii and iii
- b) i and iii
- c) ii and iii
- d) ii, iii and iv

**23) What is the purpose of a public inquiry?**
- a) To give the public the chance to voice their opinions on important issues that concern them.
- b) To give the government the opportunity to absolve itself of responsibility.
- c) To draw conclusions in order that errors committed do not happen again, to ensure public confidence and to ascertain responsibility.
- d) To call to account persons who have behaved in a negligent manner.

**24) Which one is NOT a private type ombudsman?**
- a) Financial Ombudsman
- b) Motor Ombudsman
- c) Rail Ombudsman
- d) Parliamentary and Health Service Ombudsman

**25) Which one is NOT an advantage of having a Tribunal system?**
- a) Cheaper
- b) Faster
- c) Lack of precedent
- d) Legally binding, but less formal and fair process

# ANSWERS

### Part A - CONSTITUTIONAL LAW

1) c; 2) b; 3-) d; 4) d; 5) a; 6) b; 7) a; 8) d; 9) c; 10) d; 11) c; 12) b; 13) d; 14) d; 15) a; 16) a; 17) a; 18) d; 19) a; 20) a, b, c; 21) b; 22) a; 23) a; 24) d; 25) b

### Part B – HUMAN RIGHTS

1) a; 2) d; 3-) a; 4) d; 5) d; 6) a; 7) c; 8) c; 9) d; 10) d; 11) b; 12) a; 13) c; 14) c; 15) b; 16) a; 17) a; 18) d; 19) a; 20) d; 21) c; 22) d; 23) a; 24) c; 25) d

### Part C – ADMINISTRATIVE LAW

1) c; 2) d; 3-) d; 4) d; 5) a; 6) a; 7) c; 8) d; 9) c; 10) c; 11) c; 12) d; 13) d; 14) c; 15) b; 16) b; 17) a; 18) a; 19) d; 20) a; 21) b; 22) a; 23) c; 24) d; 25) c

1-c ✓
2-b
3-✓
4-
5-b
8-

# RECOMMENDED READING LIST

Allen, M. and Thompson, B., *Cases and Materials on Constitutional and Administrative Law* 10th ed., Oxford University Press, 2011.

Aristotle, *The Politics,* Penguin, 2000.

Bagehot, W., *The English Constitution*, Chapman and Hall, 1867.

Barnett, H., *Constitutional and Administrative Law*, 10th ed., Routledge, 2013.

Bingham, T., *The Rule of Law*, Penguin, 2011.

Bogdanor, V., *The New British Constitution*, Hart Publishing, 2009.

BPP Law School, *Study Note on Constitutional and Administrative Law*, BPP Law School, 2018.

Clayton, R. and Tomlinson, H., *The Law of Human Rights*, Oxford, 2000.

Clements, R., *Q & A Public Law*, 3rd ed., Oxford University Press, 2020.

Çınar, Özgür Heval, *Introduction to the English Legal System: Revision Guide*, Transnational Press London, 2021.

De Smith, S.A. and Brazier, R., *Constitutional and Administrative Law*, 8th ed., Penguin London, 1998.

Dicey, A. V., *An Introduction to the Law of the Constitution*, Macmillan, 1885.

Donald, A., Gordon, J., and Leach, P., *The UK and the European Court of Human Rights,* Equality and Human Rights Commission Research report 83, 2012.

Dworkin, R., *Taking Rights Seriously*, Harvard University Press, 1977.

Dworkin, R., *A Matter of Principle*, Harvard University Press, 1985.

Elliott, M. and Thomas, R., *Public Law*, 3rd ed., Oxford University Press, 201.

Fenwick H., *Text, Cases & Materials on Public Law & Human Rights*, 3rd ed., Routledge, 2010.

Foster, S., *Q & A Human Rights & Civil Liberties*, Oxford University Press, 2016.

Fuller, L., *The Morality of Law*, Yale University Press, 1964.

Gillespie, A. and Weare, S., *The English Legal System*, 5th ed., Oxford University Press, 2015.

Giussani, E., *Constitutional and Administrative Law – Textbook Series*, Sweet & Maxwell, 2008.

Greer, S., *The Margin of Appreciation: Interpretation and Discretion under the European Convention on Human Rights*, Council of Europe, 2000.

Harris, D. and O'Boyle M., *Harris, O'Boyle & Warbrick: Law of the European Convention on Human Rights*, 4th ed., Oxford University Press, 2018.

Howard, N., *Beginning Constitutional Law,* 2nd ed., Routledge, 2016.

Howe, G., 'The management of public inquiries', *Political Quarterly* 70, (1999).

Jennings, W. I., *The Law and the Constitution*, 5th ed., University of London Press, 1960.

Kavanagh, A., *Constitutional Review under the UK Human Rights Act*, Cambridge University Press, 2009.

Kilkelly, U., *The right to respect for private and family life: A guide to the implementation of Article 8 of the European Convention on Human Rights*, Council of Europe, 2003.

Korff, D., *The Right to Life: A Guide to the Implementation of Article 2 of the European Convention on Human Rights*, Council of Europe, 2006.

Loveland, I., *Constitutional Law, Administrative Law and Human Rights: A Critical Introduction,* 8th ed., Oxford University Press, 2018.

Lyon, A., *Constitutional History of the United Kingdom*, 2nd ed., Routledge, 2016.

Macovei, M., *Freedom of Expression: A guide to the implementation of Article 10 of the European Convention on Human Rights*, Council of Europe, 2004.

Mole, N. and Harby, C., *The right to a fair trial: A guide to the implementation of Article 6 of the European Convention on Human Rights*, Council of Europe, 2006.

Munro, C.R., *Studies in Constitutional Law*, 2nd ed, Oxford University Press, 2005.

Murdoch, J., *Freedom of thought, conscience and religion: A guide to the implementation of Article 9 of the European Convention on Human Rights*, Council of Europe, 2007.

Parpworth, N., *Butterworth Core Text: Constitutional and Administrative Law*, 10th ed., Oxford University Press, 2018.

Pollard, D., Parpworth, N. and Hughes, D., *Constitutional and Administrative Law: Text with Materials*, 4th ed., Oxford University Press, 2007.

Rawls, J., *A Theory of Justice*, Oxford University Press, 1973 (revision ed. 1999).

Raz, J., *The Authority of Law*, 2nd ed., Oxford University Press, 2009.

Reidy, A., *The Prohibition of Torture: A guide to the implementation of Article 3 of the European Convention on Human Rights*, Council of Europe, 2002.

Street, A., *Judicial Review and the Rule of Law: Who is in Control?*, The Constitution Society, 2013.

Thomas, M. and McGourlay, C., *Concentrate English Legal System*, Oxford University Press, 2017.

Wadham, J., Mountfield, H., Gallagher, C. and Prochaska, E., *Blackstone's Guide to the Human Rights Act 1998*, 7th ed., Oxford University Press, 2015.

Walsh, K. and Higgins, J., 'The use and impact of inquiries in the NHS', *British Medical Journal*, Vol 325, 2002.

# INDEX

# T

# U

# W